THE EARLY SOCIOLOGY OF
MANAGEMENT AND ORGANIZATIONS

THE EARLY SOCIOLOGY OF MANAGEMENT AND ORGANIZATIONS

THE EARLY SOCIOLOGY OF MANAGEMENT AND ORGANIZATIONS

Edited by Kenneth Thompson

VOLUME VI

The Human Problems of an Industrial Civilization

Elton Mayo

Routledge
Taylor & Francis Group

LONDON AND NEW YORK

First published 1933 by The Macmillan Company, New York

This edition published 2003
by Routledge
2 Park Square, Milton Park, Abingdon, Oxon, OX14 4RN

Simultaneously published in the USA and Canada
by Routledge
270 Madison Avenue, New York, NY 10016

Transferred to Digital Printing 2004

Routledge is an imprint of the Taylor & Francis Group

Copyright © 1933 by The Macmillan Company
Editorial matter and selection © 2003 Kenneth Thompson

Typeset in Times by Keystroke, Jacaranda Lodge, Wolverhampton
Printed and bound by CPI Antony Rowe, Eastbourne

British Library Cataloguing in Publication Data
A catalogue record for this book is available from the British Library

Library of Congress Cataloging in Publication Data
A catalog record for this book has been requested.

ISBN 0–415–27982–8 (set)
ISBN 0–415–27988–7 (volume VI)

Publisher's Note
The publisher has gone to great lengths to ensure the quality of this reprint
but points out that some imperfections in the original book may be apparent.

THE HUMAN PROBLEMS OF AN INDUSTRIAL CIVILIZATION

BY

ELTON MAYO

Professor of Industrial Research, Graduate School of Business Administration, Harvard University

NEW YORK
THE MACMILLAN COMPANY
1933

CONTENTS

THE HUMAN PROBLEMS OF AN INDUSTRIAL CIVILIZATION

CHAPTER I

FATIGUE

THE human aspect of industry has changed very considerably in the last fifty years. The nature and range of these changes are still partly unknown to us, but the question of their significance is no longer in dispute. Whereas the human problems of industry were regarded until recently as lying within the strict province of the specialist, it is now beginning to be realized that a clear statement of such problems in particular situations is necessary to the effective thinking of every business administrator and every economic expert. In the nineteenth century there was an ill-founded hope that some species of political remedy for industrial ills might be discovered; this hope has passed. There have been very considerable political changes, both generally and also in particular national systems, since the end of the war in 1918. But the human problems of industrial organization remain identical for Moscow, London, Rome, Paris, and New York. As ever in human affairs, we are struggling against our own ignorance and not against the machinations of a political adversary.

The belief that we need to know far more of the human aspect and human effect of industry is quite recent; it is indeed a development of the post-war years. In 1893, in England, Sir William Mather of the firm of Mather & Platt, Manchester, tried the experiment of reducing the weekly hours of work from fifty-four to

1

forty-eight. "Two years' experience proved that the change had brought about a considerable increase in production and a decrease in the amount of lost time." [1] This led to the institution of a forty-eight hour week in the arsenals and dockyards of the British government, but, apart from this, the results of the experiment "did not lead to any general adoption of analogous methods on the part of privately owned establishments."

This general disregard persisted until the outbreak of war; then attention to the matter speedily became compulsory. Apparently no one had ever sufficiently considered the enormous demand upon industry that would be exercised by a war-machine organized upon so heroic a scale; armies counted in millions were a gigantic innovation. Nor had anyone considered the effect of the strenuous and sustained exertion imposed upon those who worked to provide supplies. The authorities became aware of a "national lack of knowledge of the primary laws governing human efficiency." In particular there was a "need for scientific study of the hours of work and other conditions of labor likely to produce the maximum output at which the effort of the whole people was aimed." The report from which I quote adds that, owing to this lack of knowledge, the hours and conditions of work were generally such as to be "progressively detrimental" to the maintenance of output for long or short periods. It was in these circumstances, and as part of the organization of a nation for war, that the Health of Munition Workers Committee was first constituted in 1915, with immediate and remarkable benefit to workers generally, and to output, as a result of the inquiries then undertaken. The most frequently quoted instance of

[1] Report No. 27, Industrial Fatigue Research Board, p. iii.

such benefit is that of certain women who worked in a munition factory for twelve hours a day in 1915; in 1916 and 1917, after the constitution of the Committee, their day was reduced to ten hours. A comparison of the incidence of industrial accidents in this group showed that in 1915 accidents "were two and one-half times more numerous than in the subsequent ten-hour day period." [2]

These early investigations were necessarily limited to war conditions in industry; most of them were begun in munition factories. They were, nevertheless, "productive of results sufficiently striking in themselves, but still more so in their potential application to industries generally." [3] Consequently, when the Health of Munition Workers Committee was disbanded in 1917, the Medical Research Council and the Department of Scientific and Industrial Research acting together created the Industrial Fatigue Research Board to continue the work and to extend it "by embracing the whole of industry within its scope." In 1921, these pioneering efforts were supplemented by the institution in London of a self-supporting National Institute of Industrial Psychology "with interests and functions akin to those of the Board." The founder of this Institute, Dr. C. S. Myers, was himself a member of the Fatigue Board; he resigned from direction of the psychological laboratory in the University of Cambridge in order to give all his time to the development of the industrial inquiry. One of the chief functions of the Institute has been to hold together a group of skilled investigators who give continuous attention to certain industrial problems. In spite of his expressed dis-

[2] Health of Munition Workers Committee, No. 21, 1918, H. M. Vernon, M.D.
[3] Industrial Fatigue Research Board, No. 27.

satisfaction with this aspect of the English work,[a] Dr. Myers has in this way done much to support and extend the work of the Fatigue Board. The only other change which calls for notice in this brief historical summary is that with the publication of its tenth annual report (1930) the Board changed its name to "Industrial Health Research Board" and dropped the word "fatigue" from its title. This change will call for comment later.

I have invited the attention of readers to the chronological development of the British research for a definite reason. The situation originally is that of an acute national emergency almost unlimited in scope. Enormous armies in the field, enormous by comparison with any historic precedent, make an unprecedented demand for munitions and supplies. The industrial mechanism endeavors to support the burden of demand and staggers at its task. The partial failure is not due to ignorance of the mechanics of production; it is due to ignorance of the human conditions of sustained production. At this point biology intervenes undramatically yet with dramatic effect; industry learns how to support its burden. The situation explains the emphasis on "output" and maximum production in the early statements of the objectives sought by investigators. But although the immediate and contemporary justification of the work was clearly indicated in the increased output thus obtained, there was from the beginning no misunderstanding of the remoter ends sought. These find statement in the very titles of the first groups formed—"health of munition workers," "industrial fatigue." Thus the group of scientists called together to serve a people in a time of

[a] *The Week-End Review*, September, 1931; article, "Mind and Machinery."

national emergency earns no great meed of popular praise but nevertheless establishes its right in public opinion to continue the research it has begun. And the work which begins in a clearly defined problem of the war, which all the world can understand, continues after the war as a complex and changing study.

There seems to be small doubt that industrial fatigue was originally conceived as a somewhat simple and special study. This was even true, at least to some extent, of the investigators themselves. Physiological fatigue had been for some time the subject of laboratory inquiry, and there was at first some hope that industrial fatigue would reveal itself as directly related to these experiments. "Numerous attempts have been made to measure fatigue experimentally by laboratory methods, and these investigations have thrown much light on the nature of fatigue and its localization. They have shown that fatigue is frequently bound up with the production of various chemical products, some of which, such as sarcolactic acid, are well-defined chemical substances, whilst others, the so-called 'fatigue toxins,' are very indefinite and uncertain." Thus a contemporary statement by a very distinguished worker. There were enthusiasts at this time, for the most part not directly connected with the actual work, who saw the problem as a very simple "causal" sequence—work, fatigue, remedy—enthusiasts whose statements seemed to imply the possibility of a single chemical discovery that might banish fatigue from industry. There was indeed a contemporary suggestion that the administration of doses of acid sodium phosphate might achieve the desired end.

A close inspection of the work of the Fatigue Board puts all such conceptions out of court. After twelve years of work, the Tenth Annual Report (December, 1929) gives a list of approximately sixty monographs published by specialist investigators. These monographs are classified, first, according to subject matter and, second, according to industries studied. Under the subject-matter classification, the general headings are:

I.	Hours of Work, Rest Pauses, etc.	10	reports
II.	Industrial Accidents	5	"
III.	Atmospheric Conditions	9	" and references
IV.	Vision and Lighting	5	reports
V.	Vocational Guidance and Selection....	7	"
VI.	Time and Movement Study	10	"
VII.	Posture and Physique	4	" and references
VIII.	Miscellaneous	9	reports

Under the "Industry" classification the industries listed are mining, textiles, boot and shoe, pottery, laundry, glass, printing and leather-making; in addition to this there are studies of "light repetition work," "muscular work," and a miscellaneous group. The number and variety of the studies after twelve years are in fact so great that it is difficult to present them in a single scheme with any sort of general coherence. The single discovery, the simple remedy, the one best way, had failed to materialize. The situation that had actually revealed itself was that of multiple factors closely interrelated and all potentially important in the control of an industry.

This observation applies not only to the whole wide field of investigation; it applies to any particular investigation in the field. The attempt to measure or develop tests for physiological fatigue in industry has been attended with small success. An early report [5] states its

[5] Fourth Annual Report, December, 1924, p. 16.

approach to the problem confidently thus: *The Principles Governing Muscular Exercise.* "As is now well known,[6] when muscular work is carried out, lactic acid is formed in the muscles and the blood. This is removable by oxidation, but if present above a certain limit, inhibits further muscular activity. The balance between the formation of the lactic acid and its removal by the inspired oxygen determines the physiological state during and after exercise." The report refers to certain university studies then being carried on under the supervision of Dr. A. V. Hill. It continues by pointing out that muscular exercise may be divided into two categories. "On the one hand, as in comparatively mild exercise, the oxygen inspired may suffice to prevent the lactic acid from reaching its inhibiting concentration, in which case . . . the exercise can be carried on indefinitely. On the other hand, as in more severe exercise, the lactic acid may accumulate so rapidly that the oxygen supply, limited as it is by the capacity of the heart and lungs, is unable to deal with it, with the consequence that the body runs into 'debt' for oxygen and eventually is compelled to pause for recovery. . . . An instance of the former type consists in walking, of the latter in running at top speed, the limiting speed varying with the individual, his state of health, training and practice, and the economy with which he uses his muscles." The report proceeds to enunciate its high hopes with respect to these excellent and interesting laboratory researches. "With the progress of this work, results directly applicable to industrial work will eventually emerge, in particular in regard to the optimum speed of working, the optimum

[6] The reference is to the work of Dr. A. V. Hill, reported by him in, for example, the Lowell Lectures, 1927, and published as "Living Machinery," Harcourt, Brace & Co., New York, 1927.

length of spell, incidence of rest pauses, etc., in the case of work involving muscular effort. . . ." It goes on to mention fatigue researches (muscular) being carried on by University College, London, and by Dr. E. P. Cathcart, now Regius Professor of Physiology in the University of Glasgow.

So much for the early hope, but what of the fulfilment? Dr. C. S. Myers writing in 1925 says: "Valuable as have been the results of these laboratory inquiries into muscular and mental fatigue, they have proved far from adequate in their practical application, for the conditions of laboratory experiment are widely removed from those of work-a-day life. Muscular fatigue in the factory cannot be isolated, as in the laboratory, from such influences as skill and intelligence which depend on the proper functioning of the higher levels of the central nervous system. . . ." [7] Later, Myers speaks of "the impossibility . . . of defining industrial fatigue in a way which will warrant the application of any of the various tests that have from time to time been devised to measure it." [8] Still later he adds, "If we continue to use the term 'fatigue' in industrial conditions, let us remember how complex is its character, how ignorant we are of its full nature, and how impossible it is in the intact organism to distinguish lower from higher fatigue and fatigue from inhibition, to separate the fatigue of explosive 'acts' from the fatigue of maintaining 'attitudes,' or to eliminate the effects of varying interest, of excitement, suggestion, and the like." [9] One begins to wonder at this point whether the word "fatigue" is not itself in serious danger of being

[7] "Industrial Psychology," People's Institute Publishing Company, New York, p. 44.
[8] *Op. cit.,* p. 71.   [9] *Op. cit.,* p. 74.

overworked; it seems to be used to describe a wide variety of situations.

Similar pessimistic conclusions were expressed by Cathcart in 1928. "Before outlining the province of industrial fatigue the subject of fatigue itself requires some consideration. The term is glibly used, like that of efficiency, and yet the average man would find it hard if not wellnigh impossible to define. Fatigue is a normal physiological condition which may become pathological, and it is this aspect of the problem which must first be considered. What is meant by the term, and can the degree of fatigue be measured? The answer to the latter part of the question will be attempted first. In spite of the enormous amount of work which has been done on the subject, the reply is in the negative. Here in Glasgow, for instance, we have tried for years to devise a really reliable test, and in common with all other workers have come to the conclusion that no test has yet been devised which will permit of assessment of the state of fatigue of any subject. It is questionable, with the means at present at our command, if it will ever be possible to measure fatigue."[10] Later in the same chapter Cathcart continues: "But what about industrial fatigue? This is a subject which is no clearer than ordinary fatigue and yet, although we cannot explain its nature, it is a well-recognized condition. Probably the best general definition, which does not commit us to any explanation of its nature, is that it is a reduced capacity for doing work. There is absolutely no question about the actual existence of fatigue amongst industrial workers, not in an excessive

[10] "The Human Factor in Industry," E. P. Cathcart, p. 17, Oxford University Press, 1928.

form but as the inevitable result of the performance of everyday work. It is, of course, obvious that if there is no satisfactory direct method for determining the degree of fatigue experimentally produced, with the majority of the contributing factors under control, no direct test for the determination of industrial fatigue can be possible at present."

"Indirectly, the problem has been very fully studied, and some, at least, of the deductions which have been drawn are undoubtedly correct and are of very considerable value. Some of the tests which have been employed indirectly to assess the degree of fatigue are:

1. Variations in output and quality of work done.
2. Lost time.
3. Labor turnover.
4. Sickness and mortality.
5. Accidents.
6. Degree of effort expended.

"Of all these indirect tests, probably the most reliable on the whole is that which measures performance or rate of output." [11] Cathcart qualifies this statement by pointing out the extreme difficulty of experiment in industry owing to, first, the great number of factors operative in an industrial situation and, second, the extreme difficulty of keeping constant conditions other than that under observation.

In a much later paper, read before a section of the British Association—the Committee on Industrial Cooperation—at the Centenary Meeting in 1931, Cathcart makes an observation which serves to dispel much of the confusion which has gathered about the term "fatigue."

[11] *Op. cit.,* pp. 20, 21.

He remarks that fatigue "cannot be defined as a single limited entity." [12]

In the Harvard Fatigue Laboratory in recent years certain inquiries have been made by Dr. L. J. Henderson and his colleagues into the biochemical changes which occur in the blood stream during active muscular exercise. Their work has been fully reported in various scientific journals and in Henderson's latest book. [13] The inquiry may be said to be based upon a developed conception of experimental method in biology which by its nature avoids the assumption that fatigue is a "single limited entity" characteristic of a simple causal series of events.

"In organic processes," says Henderson, "cause-and-effect analysis leads, in general, to erroneous conclusions. The only alternative . . . is mutual, dependence analysis which is, in general, impossible without the use of mathematics." [14] Living organism is best conceived as a number of variables in equilibrium with each other in such a fashion that a change in any one will induce changes throughout the whole organization. Biological experiment accordingly should not seek to change a factor *a* while keeping factors *b c d* . . . *n* constant, for this is impossible. [15] If factors *b c d* are put under constraint in a balanced system, the constraint will affect *a* also. For Henderson, scientific control in biological experiment means not constraint but measurement. The living organism responds to changes as a totality; in order to know the general nature of the response it is necessary to measure simultaneously as many specified variables as

[12] "Business and Science," the Sylvan Press, p. 111.
[13] "Blood," L. J. Henderson, Yale University Press.
[14] Henderson, L. J., "An Approximate Definition of Fact," University of California Publications in Philosophy, Vol. XIV, March, 1932, p. 183.
[15] *Science,* February 8, 1929, Raymond Pearl.

possible—"as few as we may, as many as we must." Thus may be gained a knowledge of the relation of the lesser changes to each other and to the general change. This method goes far towards conquest of the difficulty of "control" in biological experiment specified by Cathcart.

The first series of Harvard Fatigue Laboratory experiments which I describe are an application of this method to elucidation of the changes which occur in different individuals, of normal health, during the performance of the same task. The task in question was that of running at a rate of nearly six miles an hour upon the laboratory treadmill for a period of about twenty minutes. These experiments have been fully reported in the *Journal of Physiology* [16] as "Studies in Muscular Activity." I show here three charts prepared by Dr. D. B. Dill of the Fatigue Laboratory to illustrate the difference between certain of the experimental subjects in respect to selected variables simultaneously measured during the experiment.

The first diagram shows the effect of running at the specified rate upon an athlete in training, athletes not in training, and untrained runners. The changes shown are those which occur in the concentration of lactates and bicarbonates in the blood stream. A. V. Hill in his Lowell Lectures described the manner in which a muscular fatigue may be induced by increased concentration of lactic acid in the blood stream during exercise and the consequent diminution of the "alkali reserve," the total bicarbonates. [17] This condition culminates in "oxygen-debt" and inability to continue running. Looking at the diagram, we can see, at the extreme left, that the blood

[16] Vol. LXVI, No. 2, October 10, 1928.
[17] "Living Machinery," A. V. Hill, pp. 136 *ff*.

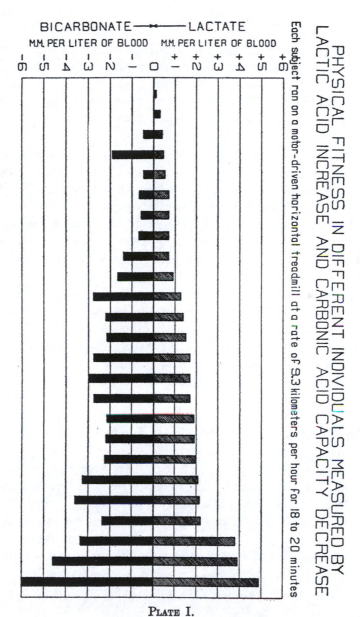

PHYSICAL FITNESS IN DIFFERENT INDIVIDUALS MEASURED BY LACTIC ACID INCREASE AND CARBONIC ACID CAPACITY DECREASE

Each subject ran on a motor-driven horizontal treadmill at a rate of 9.3 kilometers per hour for 18 to 20 minutes

BICARBONATE —⋈— LACTATE

M.M. PER LITER OF BLOOD   M.M. PER LITER OF BLOOD

Harvard Fatigue Laboratory—Dr. D.B.Dill

PLATE I.

stream of the athlete, a Marathon runner of distinction, shows virtually no change from the resting condition. His "alkali reserve" is undiminished, the lactate increase is negligible. The next two were formerly athletes and, although athletes in the strict sense no longer, are by no means completely "out of training." At the extreme right of the diagram are those who have never trained for running. It is rather interesting to know, with respect to the group of persons involved as subjects in this experiment, that the older men are grouped at the left. It happens that the best in the group, the athlete, was forty at the time of the experiment; the worst, at the extreme right, was a boy of eighteen. This does not lead, of course, to consideration of the effect of age, but leads rather to consideration of the effect of physical training.

The second diagram shows the remarkable difference as between one subject and another in respect of pulse rate during muscular exercise. At the extreme left, again, is the famous athlete of forty years; his pulse rate does not rise above approximately one hundred to the minute during the run. At the right is depicted the consequence to an untrained individual; his pulse rate quickens to one hundred and ninety and he is forced by exhaustion to give up after six minutes' exercise.

The third diagram illustrates the net oxygen consumption per kilogram of body weight by the various runners. Here again an exceedingly interesting observation emerges. The measurements show that the better runner actually consumes less oxygen; in other words, he uses less muscular effort to accomplish the same task—skill in running is characterized by economy of effort.

"From the standpoint of the efficiency of the body as a machine, final analysis of the data above presented

RELATIVE PHYSICAL FITNESS
IN DIFFERENT INDIVIDUALS
MEASURED BY PULSE RATE IN EXERCISE

Each subject ran at a rate of 5.8 miles per hour for 18 minutes, except #12 who quit because of exhaustion after 6 minutes

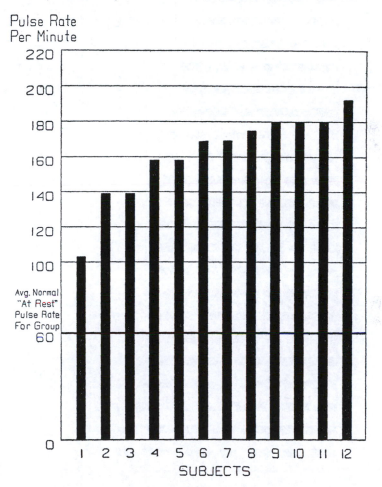

Harvard Fatigue Laboratory – Dr. D. B. Dill

PLATE II.

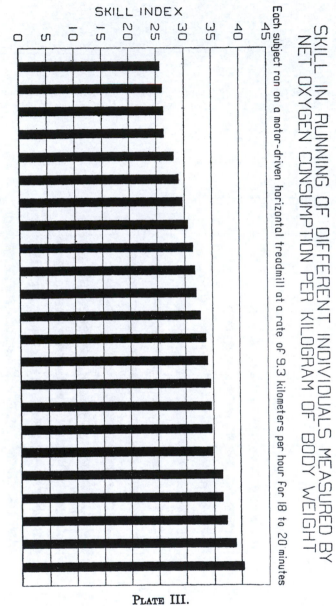

SKILL IN RUNNING OF DIFFERENT INDIVIDUALS MEASURED BY NET OXYGEN CONSUMPTION PER KILOGRAM OF BODY WEIGHT

Each subject ran on a motor-driven horizontal treadmill at a rate of 9.3 kilometers per hour for 18 to 20 minutes

SKILL INDEX

Harvard Fatigue Laboratory—Dr. D.B Dill

PLATE III.

shows the great advantage accruing to the organism as a result of physical training. The superiority of the athlete lies in his ability to meet the demand for oxygen, enabling him to maintain an internal environment varying within narrow limits only from the resting state. It is a well-established principle in physiology that function and use go hand in hand. The increased metabolism resulting from muscular exercise is met effectively only in the trained subject, through the coördination of a number of factors, the response, in general, being about what might be expected in a well-integrated system accustomed to such demands. Certain variables in the system have been measured and approximations can be made as to the relative importance of these. . . ."

"Physical training increases the lung capacity, induces a slow pulse rate, increases the stroke volume of the heart, reduces systemic blood pressure during work, and probably greatly increases the capillary diffusion area in the muscles as it does in the lungs. Coördination of these and other unknown factors by the nervous system results in the provision of an adequate supply of oxygen to meet the needs of the organism up to levels of relatively severe work, with the maintenance of optimum conditions within the body for long periods of time. In the untrained subject, these mechanisms may be said to be relatively undeveloped." [18] The tendency in the untrained subject is for him "to reach maximum pulse and respiratory rates at levels of work that produce almost no embarrassment for the athlete."

These experiments have a high interest for biochemistry, physiology, and medicine because of the facts

[18] "Dynamical Changes Occurring in Man at Work," A. V. Bock, D. B. Dill, and others, *Journal of Physiology*, Vol. LXVI, No. 2, Oct. 10, 1928, p. 159.

elicited with respect to the organic exchanges during muscular activity. They have a high interest also as illustrative of an important innovation in biological technique. Their indirect consequences for industrial and human investigation will be presented subsequently. At the moment it is necessary to point out that although a particular form of organic unbalance (which Hill has termed fatigue) is here specified clearly in many of its aspects and is measured, there is yet no very direct application to industry. This type of disequilibrium or fatigue might, and perhaps occasionally does, occur in industry; but in fact its occurrence is rare or non-existent and for two reasons. The first is the commonplace that increasingly in industry the machine does the work and man merely directs it. The second reason is that where industry still demands muscular effort there is a tendency to develop a species of natural selection of those who, like the athlete in training, can undertake the work without any significant disturbance of organic balance. This is accomplished in normal times by what is known as "labor turnover"; those who find the work unduly distressing leave it. In other industrial situations where special muscular effort is not required this type of natural selection is wasteful by comparison with systematic vocational selection. But where "oxygen debt" is involved a natural selection works sufficiently well.

The experiments so far reported do not, however, by any means completely record the inquiries of the Fatigue Laboratory which possess a special significance for industry. Another series of experiments is concerned with the effect of external temperature upon capacity for continuing muscular work. In these experiments several subjects did the same work on the bicycle ergometer, first, in a laboratory room with an "external" temperature (*i.e.* external to the individual) of about 50° F., and, second, in a similar situation with an external temperature of about 90° F. There was no air movement and the humidity (fifty per cent) was approximately constant. Internal body temperature (rectal temperature) was observed frequently by means of a thermocouple and "heart rate was recorded continuously with a cardiotachometer."

Observations on the rate of increase of body temperature showed that, after a small initial rise, a constant temperature was soon reached, if conditions for heat dissipation were favorable; "otherwise body temperature rises until exhaustion intervenes."

"The heart rate increases with external temperature even when internal temperature is the same. Its output per unit time may remain constant or increase slightly. Consequently, its output per beat must diminish with increasing external temperature. Blood supply to the skin and inactive muscles increases and to active muscles probably diminishes with increasing external temperature."

"In our experiments four of the five subjects became exhausted at the high temperature when doing work which they carried on easily at a low temperature. Yet there was no considerable lactic acid accumulation in the body as a whole, no exhaustion of fuel reserves, and there was a large reserve of pulmonary ventilation. The most probable hypothesis for explaining these data is that the heart muscle itself had reached the limit of its capacity, for it had attained its maximum rate while no other part of the organism was working at capacity."

"The implications of these experiments are many, for physical activity is often carried on under conditions un-

HEART RATE

Results of Exercise on an Ergometer

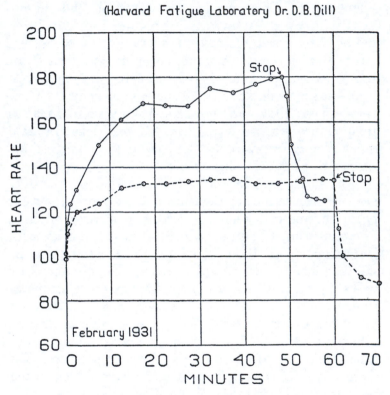

(Harvard Fatigue Laboratory Dr. D. B. Dill)

In a hot room, no air movement (approx. 95°F.) ———

In a cold room (approx. 50°F.) -------------

same subject in both tests

PLATE IV.

favorable to heat dissipation. The leisurely habits of those who live in the tropics have a sound basis in physiological necessity." [19]

These experiments illustrate and measure certain variables in relation to a second, and different, type of organic unbalance which, although it differs from the first, may nevertheless operate equally to make continuance of work impossible. The implications for industry are again many, as the authors suggest; there is here, however, a direct application also. In a certain factory the operation of changing an electrode is accompanied by an almost inevitable partial exposure of the workers to the heat of the electric furnace. Cases of heat exhaustion occur almost invariably in the summer when the shade temperature outside the factory is between 90 and 100 degrees Fahrenheit, practically never in the winter when the external temperature may be between zero and freezing point Fahrenheit. According to the medical officer in charge these heat exhaustions are characterized in the factory as in the laboratory by an increased body temperature (102° F.) and a rapid pulse rate—160 or above.

During the summer of 1932 Dr. D. B. Dill and Dr. J. H. Talbott, of the Fatigue Laboratory, visited the construction works at Boulder Dam in order to pursue further their researches into the effect upon the human organism of exertion in high summer temperatures. Their experimental findings have not yet been published, but among such findings is one of considerable interest for industry and for us. Instances occur in such a work situation of a curious form of heat prostration accompanied by muscular "cramps." This may, in individual cases,

[19] Arbeitsphysiologie; 4. Band, 6. Heft. "Physical Performance in Relation to External Temperature." D. B. Dill, H. T. Edwards, and others, 1931, pp. 517, 518.

lead to quite serious illness. I cannot speak of the many factors involved and of the individual differences, but the critical finding is that in such cases there has been an excessive loss of sodium chloride (common salt) through profuse perspiration. The appropriate administration of common salt goes far to get rid of the "cramps" and to restore the individual to normality.

It is possible at this point to return to consideration of the many and various meanings that are confused in the term "fatigue." Physiologists who work in the industrial field—H. M. Vernon, E. P. Cathcart—are clear of this confusion; those who read their published works are not. Current business theory bases itself on a very simple assumption, which economic theory seems to justify. This assumption is that "work" is something that is "taken out of" the worker; wages are paid him as compensation for the vaguely conceived loss. Wages are paid by time, consequently the loss must be continuous; perhaps some such conception of a continuous loss is at the root of the business-economic idea of "fatigue." It is, of course, possible to support such an idea by special pleading. One might say, for example, that all physiological "work" consumes fuel reserves and that after a working day such reserves are at least in some degree depleted. The objection to this is that it does not in any sense represent the problems actually encountered in industry or in the physiological laboratory. The physiologist—Hill or Vernon, Henderson or Dill—is describing, and measuring, a situation in which some defect of external relation is giving rise to an organic unbalance in the individual "worker." This unbalance is not "fatigue" in the sense that it is the same organic ill in all situations. On the contrary, its nature depends upon both the external con-

dition and the individual. Of the infinitude of such mal-
adaptations, we have looked at three—muscular activity
in an untrained subject and "oxygen-debt," insufficient
air movement in a hot room and heart inefficiency in
exercise, excessive loss of sodium chloride in perspiration
and muscular "cramps." In every instance there is some
"interference" with the balanced relation of the variables
involved in bodily activity. And the disaster is not slowly
continuous as the wage theory implies; once it has
appeared, the individual is rapidly forced to stop work.

On the other hand, the physiologists equally describe
and measure situations in which the individual continues
to perform the task set him—even under the experimental conditions. In such instances, they point out, he
achieves a "steady state." He is equal to the task, his
inner equilibrium is maintained at the higher expendi-
ture of energy. "Similarly during continuous muscular
exercise a 'steady state' is reached when the demand for
oxygen is adequately met. Such a steady state implies
a relatively constant total ventilation, elimination only
of carbon dioxide produced in metabolism, steady pulse
and respiratory rates and a constant internal environment." [20] Given that an individual can achieve this
steady state, one is entitled to expect that "optimum conditions within the body" will be maintained "for long
periods of time." [21]

That the problem of modern industry is akin to these
findings, but does not lie wholly, or even chiefly, in the
area of gross organic unbalance can easily be illustrated
by reference to certain measurements made by the department of industrial research of Harvard University in

[20] *Journal of Physiology*, Vol. LXVI, No. 2, Art. 10, 1928, p. 162.
[21] *Ibid.*, p. 159.

AVERAGE FIGURES FOR PULSE PRODUCT AND OTHER DATA FOR DIFFERENT FACTORY GROUPS

Rank	Type of Work	Position	Working Day Hrs.-Min.	Sex	Pulse Product Average
1	Inspect and fold clothing	Standing-no moving about	8-45	Female	41
2	Machine shop	Various	8-45	Male	41
3	Coil winding	Sitting	8-45	Female	39
4	Coil winding	Sitting	8-45	Female	36
5	Mule spinning	Standing and walking	8-45	Male	35
6	Mica splitting	Sitting	9-45	Female	35
7	Bench hands electrical apparatus	Sitting	9-45	Female	31
8	Power sewing machines	Sitting	8-45	Female	31
9	Stenographers, task and bonus system	Sitting	7-25	Female	31
10	Relay assembly (test room; no rest periods	Sitting	8-45	Female	31
11	Gaiter conveyor	Sitting	7-30	Female	30
12	Winding (textile mill).	Standing and sitting	8-45	Female	29
13	Quarter room, rubber shoe factory; piecework	Standing-many interruptions	9-00	Female	29
14	Stenographers, weekly salary	Sitting	7-30	Female	28
15	Stenographers, weekly salary	Sitting	7-00	Female	27
16	Shoe conveyor (rubbers)	Standing and sitting	8-10	Female	26
17	Relay assembly (test room; two rest periods	Sitting	8-45	Female	26
18	Quarter room, rubber shoe factory; team work	Sitting	7-30	Female	26
19	Rubber shoe makers (bench); team work	Standing and sitting	8-00	Female	26
20	Stitching machines, rubber shoe factory	Sitting	7-30	Female	24
21	Shoe conveyor (rubbers)	Standing and sitting	8-10	Female	23
22	Shoe conveyor (rubbers)	Standing and sitting	8-10	Female	23
23	Gaiter makers (bench; team work	Standing and sitting	8-00	Female	23

Adapted From: "The Quantitative Measurement of Human Efficiency under Factory Conditions", O.S.Lovekin - Journal of Industrial Hygiene, April 1930, No. XII-4

$$\text{Pulse Product} = \frac{\text{Pulse Rate} \times \text{Pulse Pressure}}{100}$$

where Pulse Pressure = Systolic Pressure minus Diastolic Pressure

PLATE V.

collaboration with the Fatigue Laboratory. It will have been noticed by readers that in those instances where an individual subject is being forced to "give up" what he is doing, his pulse rate and blood pressures are adversely affected. These symptoms serve as signals of what is happening, although they do not reveal its nature. (For example, pulse rate rises equally as a signal of oxygen-debt and of the external temperature heart inefficiency.) It is therefore possible by taking serial readings of pulse rate and blood pressures periodically in a working day to determine sufficiently whether the workers in a given department are working in a "steady state" or not. Two papers by O. S. Lovekin upon measurements of "pulse product" (pulse pressure multiplied by pulse rate) under laboratory conditions and in factories serve to show that different types of work call for different expenditures of energy, but that, upon the whole, factory workers exhibit low and steady pulse products. That is to say, they seem to do their work organically in a "steady state." [22]

The physiological conception of work pays small tribute, therefore, to the business-economic theory. Work can be done only in a steady state; interruption comes, in any ordinary industrial situation, not from any partial exhaustion of fuel reserves but from some "interference." This interference is of the nature of an external condition which carries as a consequence for certain individuals an actual organic disequilibrium which makes continuation of effort for such individuals impossible.

"We can say that fatigue is not an entity but merely a convenient word to describe a variety of phenomena. The common fallacy of supposing that the word 'fatigue'

[22] *Journal of Industrial Hygiene*, "Quant. Measurement of Human Efficiency Under Factory Conditions," O. S. Lovekin, Vol. XII, pp. 99-120, 153-167.

corresponds to a definite thing has been the source of much confusion. Fatigue from short bursts of activity, whether by the whole body or by isolated muscle groups, is characterized by increase in lactic acid and temporary inability to continue. Fatigue from depletion of fuel reserves does not occur commonly in man, but when it does, chemical analysis of the blood reveals a low level of blood sugar. Fatigue from working in a hot environment has several manifestations, the most simple to measure being an increase in heart rate. Finally, of two individuals doing the same task one may be more fatigued than the other because the poor nervous coördination of the unskillful man makes it necessary for him to expend more energy than the other. In general, fatigue from any of these causes is greater the more nearly the individual approaches his capacity for work." [23]

We cannot be surprised, then, that the English Research Board has dropped the word "fatigue" from its title. It is too fatally easy to conclude that because we have a word "fatigue" there must be a simple thing or fact that corresponds with it—a common fallacy discussed by Henderson in his studies of Pareto. [24] The industrial investigator is constantly forced in his inquiries to take account of many factors in a complex situation; wherever the general effect is unsatisfactory to the worker and to industry he sets himself to discover the nature of the disequilibrium and the nature of the interference. The monographs published by the scientific workers under the Fatigue Board do not discuss fatigue directly; they inquire into hours of work and rest-pauses, atmospheric conditions, vision and lighting, vocational

[23] D. B. Dill; Personnel, Am. Management Asscn., May, 1933.
[24] *"Traité de Sociologie Générale,"* Pareto, Vol. I, p. 568, par. 1071.

selection (*i.e.* individual differences with respect to a particular task), posture and physique and so on.

But the value of this method and conception is not confined to physiology. The interferences which occur in industry and disturb it are not all of the nature of organic hazards.

CHAPTER II

WHAT IS MONOTONY?

THE physiologists have found that work can continue to be performed only in a "steady state." For them this means that the organism can respond to external effort only for so long as an inner equilibrium is maintained between a large number of mutually dependent variables. Dr. W. B. Cannon speaks of this condition as "homeostasis," an equivalence between the "interofective" and "exterofective" factors.[1] Given that a steady state is achieved, "the exercise can be carried on indefinitely."[2] If an individual is unable to carry on and if this inability is organically conditioned, then some external condition or some internal incapacity is interfering to prevent interofective support of exterofective action.

The industrial investigation has from the beginning been compelled to recognize that the interferences which operate to prevent sustained work in industry are not merely or mainly organic. An early report, 1924, of the Fatigue Board in discussing the effect of systematically arranged rest-pauses says: "Rest-pauses must clearly be treated from two points of view according to the nature of the work. In muscular work they must be regarded mainly as rests in the literal sense; that is, they serve as recovery periods from the effects of physiological fatigue.

[1] "The Wisdom of the Body," W. B. Cannon. New York, W. W. Norton & Co., Inc.
[2] Industrial Fatigue Research Board, Fourth Annual Report, p. 16.

28

On the other hand, in work of which the main feature is repetition rather than effort, boredom and monotony are the factors to be taken into account rather than fatigue, and here the action of the rest-pauses probably depends on change from the main occupation rather than on complete cessation from work. The two problems, therefore, are quite distinct and ought to be studied independently." [3] The problem of monotony as clearly distinct from fatigue owes its definition chiefly to Dr. H. M. Vernon, one of the senior investigators of the original Health of Munition Workers Committee and of the Board. In the year 1924 he published two monographs, one a study of rest-pauses in industry, the other some observations on the effects of variety in repetitive work. [4] Mr. S. Wyatt, who has since developed the study further, was associated with both inquiries. The former of these monographs consists of two studies, the first by Vernon and Bedford, industrial; the second by Wyatt, experimental. The industrial study is thus summarized: "Estimation of the effect of introducing rest-pauses (five to ten minutes) during the work spells is very difficult, because other influences cannot be excluded. . . . However, the rests were followed by a slight but genuine improvement of output in most of the instances investigated, even after making a full allowance for the effect of practice. . . . The rest-pause effect takes several months to reach its full extent."

"Apart from regularized rest-pauses, the workers always get a certain amount of change (a) by taking voluntary rests from work, and (b) owing to the fact that they have to fetch and carry material, and do other jobs

---

[3] Industrial Fatigue Research Board, Fourth Annual Report, p. 697.
[4] Industrial Fatigue Research Board, No. 25, H. M. Vernon, T. Bedford, S. Wyatt; No. 26, H. M. Vernon, S. Wyatt, A. D. Ogden.

which afford relief from the monotony of their chief occupation." [5] Wyatt, as a result of his experimental study uncomplicated by industrial conditions, is more specific. "The objective conditions of modern industry show an increasing tendency to give rise to monotony. This is due to the increased sub-division of labor and amount of repetition work. . . . Although such objective conditions are conducive to increased monotony, the amount of monotony experienced probably depends more on the attitude of the operative towards his work. It is well known that the same industrial task has different subjective effects upon different individuals, and while some may find the work extremely monotonous and at times even intolerable, others find it comparatively pleasant, and prefer it to more varied occupations. Where, however, the work has a subjective sameness and gives rise to monotony, it has an inhibiting effect upon activity." [6] Both Vernon and Wyatt are observing output curves; both find that fatigue is not the only "interference" that diminishes production, monotony is equally effective. "The results of the experiment described in this report suggest that monotonous activities of the type under consideration cause a considerable reduction in output, which is most apparent about the middle of the spell of work. This reduction can be avoided to a certain extent by the introduction of a rest-pause of fifteen minutes' duration half-way through the spell. . . . There is an increase in output not only after the rest, but also before the rest takes place. . . ." [7]

Four years later, in 1928, the two Vernons in the course of a study of the effect of hours of work say, "The psychological effects of a rest-pause may be even greater than

[5] Industrial Fatigue Research Board, No 25, p. 19.
[6] *Ibid.*, p. 23.   [7] *Ibid.*, p. 34.

the physiological, especially for operatives engaged on monotonous repetition work. . . . It is impossible to measure the psychological effect of a rest-pause directly, but indirect evidence was obtained from a study of the labor turnover at three factories where somewhat similar work was performed at similar rates of pay." All the factories were large and well-appointed modern buildings; the weekly hours of work were nearly the same. At Factory B the labor turnover between 1923 and 1925 averaged 25 per cent on the average number of women employed, 42 per cent at Factory A, and 94 per cent at Factory C. "Labor turnover depends on such a number of different factors that it is impossible to argue closely, but it is a suggestive fact that at the factory with the lowest labor turnover the workers were given a fifteen-minute rest-pause in each work spell, during which they went to the canteen, and a free tea was provided for them in the afternoon. In the factory with the intermediate turnover the workers did not leave their places, but had a three-minute pause in which to drink the tea provided by the management, whilst in the factory with the highest turnover no rests at all were allowed, and the workers were discouraged from surreptitious feeding." [8]

Vernon summarizes thus: "The adoption of a rest-pause—with opportunity for refreshment—during work spells of five hours' duration is desirable:

> (a) for physiological reasons, dependent on the fact that there is often a period of six hours between breakfast and dinner.
> (b) for psychological reasons, dependent on the relief from monotony." [9]

[8] Two Studies on Hours of Work, No. 47, Industrial Fatigue Research Board, pp. 3-5.
[9] *Ibid.*, p. 16.

In 1929 Wyatt published the results of a study done in collaboration with J. A. Fraser of "the effects of monotony." The work reported is in part laboratory experiment and partly also direct industrial inquiry. The industrial study includes a number of different operations, all of them repetitive—winding, tobacco weighing, chocolate packing, soap wrapping. The industrial workers studied differ widely in intelligence. Wyatt's conclusions, briefly put, are that "the experience of boredom is fairly prevalent among operatives employed on repetitive processes," that "boredom causes a reduced rate of working which is particularly noticeable about the middle of the spell," that "boredom also causes a more variable rate of working" and "is responsible for an overestimation of time-intervals," which tends to be associated with a slower rate of working. Once again he finds that "the experience of boredom is largely dependent on individual characteristics and tendencies." Workers of superior intelligence are more easily bored, but are nevertheless "usually above the average in productive efficiency." "Temperamental tendencies are important determinants and need special investigation."

In addition to all this, however, he makes two comments of high interest: "The amount of boredom bears some relation to the degree of mechanization of the task. It is less liable to occur when (a) the work is entirely automatic. In such cases thought can be detached from work and directed to more interesting subjects, or utilized in conversation with other workers. If, however, the mind is not distracted in this manner, boredom can be very intense." Boredom is also less likely (b) "when attention is entirely concentrated on the task. In such cases unexpected and varied situations frequently arise.

. . . It (boredom) is most marked in semi-automatic processes which require enough attention to prevent mind-wandering but not enough for the complete absorption of mental activity." These observations can, I think, be extensively confirmed by the experiences of industry in the United States. O. S. Lovekin of the Industrial Research Department, at a time when he was making those measurements of "pulse-product" in various plants to which I referred in the last chapter, was interested to discover that some of the lowest and steadiest pulse-products —work with least effort—he encountered were those of young women working on conveyors. His opinion was that in such instances the work was at its automatic maximum and the group cheerfully social.

Wyatt's second interesting conclusion is expressed thus: "The amount of boredom experienced bears some relation to the conditions of work. It is less liable to arise (a) when the form of activity is changed at suitable times within the spell of work, (b) when the operatives are paid according to output produced instead of time worked, (c) when the work is conceived as a series of self-contained tasks rather than as an indefinite and apparently interminable activity, (d) when the operatives are allowed to work in compact social groups rather than as isolated units, and (e) when suitable rests are introduced within the spell of work." [10]

At this point it is wise to pause for a moment in order to make certain that we do not misunderstand the observations of Vernon and Wyatt. The word "monotony," no less than the word "fatigue" arouses reminiscences in all of us which make it easy for us to assume that there must

[10] Industrial Fatigue Research Board, No. 56, "The Effects of Monotony in Work," S. Wyatt and J. A. Fraser assisted by F. B. L. Stock, pp. 42, 43.

be a simple fact that corresponds with the word. Because
we have ourselves known what it is to be "tired" and
"bored," we tend to assume an identity of personal attitude in all the industrial situations where a fall in output
is recorded in the middle of a working spell, or a high
labor turnover over a period of time. Yet the fall in output and the labor turnover are facts of record; the experience of "boredom" is a highly hypothetical explanation.
I say highly hypothetical because it is clear that just as
"fatigue" is used to describe a variety of organic incapaci-
ties all externally conditioned in a different manner, so
also monotony is used to describe a variety of personal
situations, differently conditioned. Everything that Vernon and Wyatt say is designed to drive home this
caution. Cathcart, writing in 1928, echoes this claim:
"Closely allied to fatigue is another phenomenon as
obscure and difficult, viz., monotony. What do we really
understand by monotony? . . . Who decides what is
monotonous? The old adage that 'one man's meat is another man's poison' is true here. There is a large element
of the personal equation. An occupation may be perfectly
monotonous to one man, arousing only hatred and disgust, whereas another may find it soothing and suitable.
And again, what may be found monotonous one day may
not be so the next. It varies from individual to individual, and even from time to time in the same individual." [11] Psychology is beset, to an extent probably
greater than any other study, by a tendency to substitute
words for careful observation, words which rouse a vague
echo of half-remembered experiences in the hearer's
mind. We are not emancipated from the rigorous meth-

[11] "The Human Factor in Industry," E. P. Cathcart, Oxford University Press, pp. 31, 32.

ods of Henderson or Hill merely because the mutually
dependent factors in a situation have become personal
and social rather than organic, and are accordingly more
difficult of measurement. It is true that difficulty of
measurement, and consequently of precision and spe-
cificity, enormously complicate the task. It is much easier
to measure non-significant factors than to be content
with developing a first approximation to the significant.
So one finds that between the Scylla of mere argument
about words and the Charybdis of measurement of the
unimportant, much would-be psychology has run violently down a steep place into the sea.

This alarming mixture of metaphors impels me to return hastily to my discussion. From the observations of
Vernon and Wyatt, quoted above, two interesting considerations emerge. First, the capacity to be unfavorably
influenced by repetitive work differs between individuals
in respect of, for example, what can be tentatively called
intelligent endowment and temperament. Second, the
social or personal aspect of the particular industrial group
affects the situation in some way, and profoundly. Fortunately these two aspects of the study have received
capable attention from two investigators of the Fatigue
Board; I refer to the work of May Smith and Millais
Culpin.

Miss Smith makes her first contribution to the inquiry
into the social determinants of individual activity in a far
too little-known essay upon "General Psychological Problems Confronting an Investigator" published as early as
1924.[12] Her statement is so excellent that I quote it at
some length. "It is more than probable," she says, that

[12] Industrial Fatigue Research Board, Fourth Annual Report,
pp. 26 *ff.*

a student of industrial conditions "will be confronted with the problems of the general sameness of the work and the effect of this on individual workers. The word most commonly used to describe this sameness is monotony; this is often uncritically assumed to be synonymous with 'repetition of movement' and the reason is not far to seek. The person usually employed in criticizing or describing industrial processes belongs to a class which is unaccustomed to remain long hours at purely repetitive work. When observing workers so employed, he therefore tends to imagine what he would feel like in such a position, to project his own feelings on to the worker, and to stigmatize the process as monotonous. His verdict may or may not be true; its truth or falsity depends on the worker.

"Literally, 'monotonous' means 'one tone'; it suggests absence of change, a flat wash, a dead level, a situation which fails to provide for the person any intellectual stimulus or emotional change. For the realization of change two factors are necessary: (a) an actual objective change; (b) a person who can be affected by it. The most exciting situations would fail to be appreciated as such by certain melancholic individuals. Repetitive processes, therefore, must either be studied as such, or else put in their complete setting, which setting would include, at least, the repetitive work, the varying amount done as the hours go on, the opinion of fellow-workers and the authorities with regard to that work, physiological changes with regard to meals, fatigue, etc., emotional changes . . . and the collective life of the factory. *The total reaction at any given moment will be a reaction to a composite situation which does not remain unchanged. The consciousness of one or other factor of the com-*

*posite situation varies from person to person and even
from time to time in the same person."* [13]

Miss Smith develops the theme of individual differences with respect to monotony, then returns to her main
topic: "The writer had recently to spend some time in
two factories doing the same repetitive work; in the one
there were many complaints of dullness, in the other
none; in the one the majority of faces expressed a dull
acquiescence in existence, in the other, the general joy
and happiness in the work was obvious. If a study of
repetitive work done in these two factories had followed
the same lines, the result would have been different. In
the one, no one apparently took any interest in the
workers, there was no esprit de corps and a general slack-
ness prevailed; to get the week's money was the only interest and that is bound to be a fitful interest. In the
other there was not only a real interest in the work, in
the accumulation of it as the day wore on, but also a desire to win the approval of the authorities and interest in
many social activities binding one to another. *The repetitive work is a thread of the total pattern, but is not
the total pattern.*[14]

"Another point of view sometimes overlooked is that
there are compensations in many processes, if one studies
the worker as a human being and not only as a performer
of a repetition process. . . . The adoption of particular
machines by particular workers and their dislike of a
temporary removal reveal an interest in the machines as
such, which an observer when judging the work might
easily overlook, but which cannot, without falsifying the
account, be omitted.

[13] *Loc. cit.,* p. 29; italics mine, E. M.
[14] Italics mine, E. M.

"The worker on repetitive processes may be repeating a very limited number of movements, but his emotional life may be quite varied; he has to adjust to superiors, to equals, to subordinates; if he fails to please the first he may find sympathy and support from the others; he has an audience so that even a tyrannical foreman does not exert an unmodified influence. It is difficult to assess a situation which comprises from the point of view of a worker, at least, the sense of injustice resulting from the careless criticisms of a superior, the feeling of support from one's fellow workers' sympathy, the *esprit de corps* in allying with them against the superior, while to certain characters the joy of having a grievance is incalculable. When such situations arise—and they are not rare—the focus of interest would go from the monotony of the work to the emotion aroused." Miss Smith then describes how praise from a superior while arousing another type of emotion may nevertheless similarly move the focus of interest from the repetitive work to the social situation. She continues: "Days vary in length, as every worker knows, and ten hours of one day are shorter than eight or nine of another. *The work remains the same; it is the general situation and the individual emotional changes that vary.*[15] So many descriptions of factory conditions are like skeleton outlines, or those wire reproductions of the correct movements for motion study; they are quite true, but they lack humanity."

"It is not intended to suggest that repetitive work is good in itself; the point is that an investigator of repetitive work will find himself constantly faced with these personal problems which ought not to be neglected. The mechanical point of view is the result of this neglect."

"The point of view which looks upon a person as a

[15] Italics mine, E. M.

kind of extension to a machine is sometimes implicit, even in discussions on intelligence. Those responsible for selecting people sometimes talk as if the problem of selection were merely that of finding .out: (a) the degree of intelligence required for a particular job; (b) the person with that degree. While it is probably true that such an adaptation might bring about a more harmonious relationship than where the two did not fit, yet a problem of equal importance is the study of emotional differences. . . . Where the activity concerned involves highly developed attention or a limited set of delicate adjustments, mental conflicts, conscious or unconscious, will be more likely to interfere with the success of the work than where the movements are cruder and the registration of changes less refined. Doubtless, the best thing to do would be to cure the sufferer, but while this is a counsel of perfection it is at least desirable and more possible to direct his activities into channels where a feeling of inefficiency with its attendant depression is not added to the original weakness. Intelligence alone is not the only criterion of success."

Finally Miss Smith returns to the very important question as to the assumptions an industrial investigator should make, the method he should use. "Dr. Cyril Burt has described very aptly in discussing juvenile delinquency what he calls 'multiple determination,' *i.e.* that a particular result is not caused by some one factor operating equally on all people, so that the presence of this factor invariably would produce the same result. Rather is it that there are several factors which together, operating on a particular temperament, will produce the result." [16] It is clear that before we can profitably assess the

[16] Industrial Fatigue Research Board, Fourth Annual Report, pp. 29–32.

part played in industrial determinations by something termed "monotony," we need to be accurately informed with respect to (a) external working conditions, (b) the social-personal situation in its relation to the individuals concerned, and (c) individual differences of capacity and temperament.

Millais Culpin and May Smith demonstrated the importance of their method in an inquiry into the incidence of telegraphists' cramp, a report of which was published by the Board in 1927. Dr. Culpin is an authority upon the psychoneuroses and it is probable that the original intention of the study was, at least in part, to discover a simple means of excluding from telegraphic work persons liable to develop the disability. The issue of the investigation proved to have an interest far above this; in effect it illustrates a method by which the different individual "boredoms" may be further analyzed and in some instances resolved.

The method of inquiry is simply described. "To study a subject merely as the doer of a particular piece of work is of little value; the work to the worker is part of a whole, made up of his numerous reactions to situations, real and ideal, over and above his work. Sometimes it is the phantasy life that is of more importance to the individual than the apparent real life. It is clearly impossible to obtain a thorough knowledge of anyone, but *it has proved possible to get the point of view of a subject with sufficient clearness to yield an insight into the relation of the work he does to his general attitude to life.*" [17]

The investigators point out that, whereas it is now

[17] "A Study of Telegraphists' Cramp," Smith, Culpin, and Farmer, Industrial Fatigue Research Board, No. 43, p. 17. Italics mine, E. M.

comparatively easy to assess by means of "tests" a subject's general intelligence, "there are no reliable objective methods" of determining other important qualities of his personal make-up. They, therefore, use the method of the clinical interview, "reliance has to be placed on the observation and interpretation of a doctor experienced in such work." "The method adopted was somewhat as follows :

"(i) General observation of the subject (*i.e.* the individual) such as we are all accustomed to make.

"(ii) Guided by the knowledge of many subjects (individuals), the external behavior and appearance were linked up to the mental state of which they were probably the expression.

"(iii) By questions framed so as to bring up different situations in life, it was possible to study the subject more fully and accurately, and thereby verify, disprove, or modify the earlier impression."

"It often happened that when once started the subject would give a very detailed personal account of himself, in which case the investigator would not interfere with questions." [18]

In presenting their conclusions, the investigators inquire "why telegraphy should have a 'cramp' when other occupations of an allied nature have not." We would suggest that the exacting nature of the work, the inevitable rigidity of the conditions, the isolation of this one symptom, with its disabling effects, have all operated to concentrate attention into this channel. The type likely to get cramp may have a nervous breakdown in other occupations, but it is also probable that many who break down in telegraphy might carry on more or less efficiently under conditions more amenable to individual require-

[18] *Loc. cit.*, p. 16; italics mine, E. M.

ments. In England telegraphy is a permanent occupation, which to some is one of its attractions; in America there is more mobility of labor and the disease is hardly recognized. As against the advantage of permanence one may have to put the disadvantages of relative immobility. [19]

Telegraphy, then, has a characteristic "cramp" while "other occupations of an allied nature have not." The work is "exacting in nature" and the conditions "rigid"; but while English telegraphists are numerously plagued with the disability, American operators hardly know it. Some difference in the general situation, and not in the nature of the work, serves to bring this about—perhaps the greater "mobility of labor" in the United States in 1926. This is strongly suggestive of (a) a difference in the social industrial situation, and (b) a personal attitude characterized by mental conflict—a desire to retain the permanent job at war with an increasing aversion from the exacting work and the rigid conditions. Perhaps this is a step towards the analysis of at least one type of boredom.

I have quoted this extraordinarily interesting development in the English work at considerable length for a specific reason. In two instances which I propose to describe, industrial inquiries undertaken in the United States have been driven, step by step, to similar methods and assumptions. This is of some interest, because there was at no time during the early development of the inquiries any relation between the investigators here and in England. The first instance is a Philadelphia inquiry undertaken in the year 1923; to this I shall give what space remains in this chapter. The other instance is the

[19] *Loc. cit.,* p. 36.

five-year inquiry of the Western Electric Company at its Hawthorne Works in Chicago; description of the methods employed and the results achieved at Hawthorne will occupy the next three chapters.

In September, 1923, some of us were asked to undertake an inquiry into working conditions in the mule-spinning department of a textile mill near Philadelphia, with the object of devising methods of diminishing an exceedingly high labor turnover. This labor turnover was reported to us as being approximately 250 per cent; that is to say, the mill had to "take on" about one hundred piecers every year in order to keep approximately forty working. The difficulty tended to be most acute when the factory was most busily employed and most in need of men. The mill was very well organized; the management was unusually enlightened and humane. Four financial incentive schemes were in operation and were working well in departments other than mule-spinning. The morale and production elsewhere in the mill were satisfactory; the general labor turnover, excluding the mule-spinners, was estimated at five or six per cent. The investigation and its outcome have been fully reported elsewhere.[20] I propose here to recall a few salient features of the situation that disclosed themselves, and to add some exposition of the method of inquiry used, a method which was not fully described in previous reports.

On a first inspection, the conditions of work in the mule-spinning department did not seem noticeably inferior to the conditions of work elsewhere in the plant. The spinners, like the others, worked only five days in the week; on Saturday and Sunday the factory was

---

[20] "Revery and Industrial Fatigue," *Personnel Journal*, Vol. III, No. 8, Dec., 1924.

closed down. The working day was ten hours in length, five hours in the morning and five in the afternoon, with an interval of forty-five minutes for lunch. The work was done in long "alleys" on either side of which a machine head was operating spinning frames. The number of spinning frames operated by each machine head varied from ten to fourteen; all these frames required close watching by the "head-tender" and the "piecers" in charge. The number of piecers in an alley varied according to the type of yarn that was being spun; as a general rule there were two or three. The distance between the terminal frames was approximately thirty-five yards. The work was repetitive; the piecer walked up and down the alley twisting together broken threads. When there was a "run" of inferior yarn the work demanded vigilance and constant movement. The only variation in work was that which occurred when the machine head was stopped in order to "doff" or to replace a spool. Machine "breakdowns" of a minor character were fairly frequent.

The observations of Wyatt and Fraser, quoted above, were published in London in 1929 and accordingly were not available in Philadelphia in 1923. It is interesting, however, even at this distance in time, to look back and see how the conditions of work which had evolved in mule-spinning implied an infraction of every principle these authors state. Mule-spinning was probably, for example, a "semi-automatic process" which required enough attention to be irritating and "not enough for the complete absorption of mental activity." Beyond this, Wyatt says that boredom (interpreted to mean a general down-grade rather than up-grade mental accompaniment to work, a "minus" rather than a "plus") is less liable to arise:

(a) "When the form of activity is changed at suitable intervals within the spell of work." The twisting together of broken threads for hours at a time was only rarely interrupted by "doffing" or a machine breakdown. Neither of these interruptions was in any sense pleasant or a relief. The "carding" operation performed alongside the mules looked more "monotonous" to such external observers as those described by Miss Smith. The carding operative, however, was much better able to work in leisurely fashion, to break off and chat, to vary his day.

(b) "When the operatives are paid according to output produced instead of time worked." The spinners were paid a flat-rate wage but were offered a group bonus which up to the time of the inquiry they had never earned. This was one of the incentive schemes, alluded to above, which "worked" satisfactorily elsewhere in the factory but failed completely in the spinning department. The very fact that the bonus had never been earned by the group served to convince them (although, as subsequent developments showed, mistakenly) that an impossible standard had been set. This increased rather than diminished their irritation.

(c) "When the work is conceived as a series of self-contained tasks rather than as an indefinite and apparently interminable activity." Various expressions very generally in use amongst the operatives convinced us that they regarded their work as "an indefinite and apparently interminable activity." To which they added forceful epithets.

(d) "When the operatives are allowed to work in compact social groups rather than as isolated units." The arrangement and nature of the work precluded any sociability or conversation. Although there were two or three piecers in each alley, they were always remote from each other and isolated, unless emergency, which equally precluded sociability, brought them briefly together.

(e) "When suitable rests are introduced within the spell of work." There had been no official rests, few if any unauthorized breaks, and no suggestion of rest-pauses at the time when the inquiry began.

At the beginning of the inquiry there were difficulties of observation owing to the fact that this was merely the latest of many investigations. The men were restless under observation, and the management uneasily aware of this. At this point we were greatly helped by the collaboration of the Graduate Medical School of the University of Pennsylvania in the placing of a small dispensary in the plant with a qualified nurse in charge. This nurse could administer minor remedies or first aid but was permitted also to refer cases to the Polyclinic Hospital in Philadelphia. This was a sufficient reason for her presence, this and the fact that appropriate aid was actually provided for certain individuals in need of medical advice. But the nurse in charge, in addition to her hospital qualifications, was an expert "interviewer." The method she followed was very similar to that described above by Culpin and Smith. She found that the majority of those who visited her were glad to "give a very detailed personal account" of themselves. In all such situations she would listen carefully and would not "interfere with questions." When not occupied in her small office or clinic, she would walk in her uniform through the factory—visiting all departments but giving the greater part of her time to the workers in the spinning department. Any confidences made to her, and they were many, were regarded as inviolable and not communicated to anyone unless professional need arose. In this way she came to know the attitude and personal background of every worker on "the mules" with some detail and intimacy. She thus created a "listening post" of high value to subsequent procedure in the inquiry and, incidentally, became herself something of a social nexus for the group. It was her finding that the reflections or reveries of the workers in the spinning department were uniformly pessimistic. If any one of them was permitted to talk at length, either in the nurse's office or to her in the department, the preoccupations he expressed, whether about himself, his life, his home, or the work, appeared to be almost invariably morbid.

After some discussion of the situation and its probabilities, the management agreed to institute experimentally two or three ten-minute rest-periods in the morning and again in the afternoon for a single team of piecers, constituting about one-third of the total number. In these rest-periods the men were permitted to lie down and were instructed in the best methods of gaining the maximum of muscular relaxation. From the first the men were interested and pleased; they speedily adopted the method of rest which was advised. The experiment seemed to be in some degree successful in the sense that "morale"—whatever that may be—was generally admitted to be improved, certainly by their supervisors and even by the men themselves. This improvement, curiously, extended even to those workers in the department who were not included in the experimental team. The experiment was not really satisfactory, however, at this stage because no measurement of change, or sufficiently objective evidence, was possible. Output records were kept only for the whole group, so any difference of performance of the special team remained unknown.

In October, 1923, however, the management, pleased with the improved condition of the men, decided to extend the rest-period system to include the entire personnel of the spinning department. This had the effect of making the output records significant for the experiment, and from this time on the official daily, weekly, and monthly figures were made available to us. Unfortunately we were never able to secure the departmental records of output for the period prior to October, 1923. All that we know of this period is that the men had never earned a bonus and that the various authorities considered that their best figure for any given month was probably in the neighborhood of 70 per cent.

The first chart shows the daily productivity of the spinning department from October 1, 1923, to June 30, 1924, calculated in terms of efficiency percentage. The actual weight of yarn that is spun does not provide a satisfactory criterion of production, since a thick thread weighs more than a thin one but takes less labor per unit of weight. The Company had therefore devised a scheme by which times were set for the spinning of unit weights of the various types of yarn. The time allowed in each case was experimentally determined, allowance being made for time lost in doffing, machine breakdowns, and so on. The time allowed ranked as 100 per cent and the department was asked to make an average of 75 per cent for the working days in a month in return for the flat-rate wage paid. Beyond this the scheme provided that any month in which the group average exceeded 75 per cent man-hour efficiency on the Company scale, every worker in the group should be paid a percentage addition to his

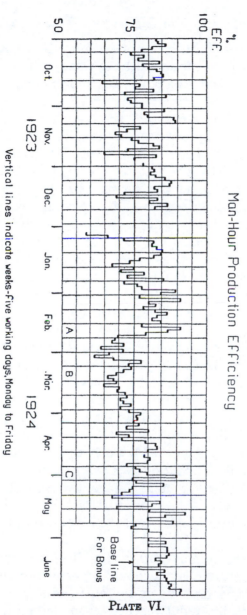

PRODUCTION - SPINNING MULES - NINE MONTHS

Man-Hour Production Efficiency

PLATE VI.

Vertical lines indicate weeks-five working days, Monday to Friday

Taken from: "Revery and Industrial Fatigue" by Elton Mayo—Journal of Personnel Research vol.Ⅲ, No.8, December 1924

ordinary wage equal to the group percentage in excess of 75. Thus an 80 per cent monthly average would have meant a 5 per cent bonus on his wages to every employee in the department.

The rest-pause innovation was accompanied, from its introduction, by an improvement in the officially recorded productive efficiency. The mental and physical condition of the men was distinctly bettered, their comments to observers were less generally pessimistic than before. Whereas the financial incentive of the bonus had not previously operated to stimulate production, the men now began to be pleased by the fact that they were working less time, earning bonuses as never before, and feeling less tired and irritated. For the first five months of the experiment, the average productive efficiency of the department was 80 per cent, the lowest month was 78¾ per cent, the highest 82.

The system was not, however, altogether satisfactory. It had occurred to someone—not an executive officer— that the rest-period idea might be improved. The men were accordingly made to "earn" their rest-periods. That is, they did not necessarily get a rest at an established time; they were allowed to rest only after completing a certain operation. This meant that they could not always anticipate a definite number of rests at stated periods. On some days, indeed, they might have two rest-periods only. Nevertheless, for the most part they had three or four such intervals in the day and the innovation worked fairly well.

This general condition continued until February 15, when, in response to a heavy demand for deliveries, some- one in the factory took it upon himself to order the rest- periods abandoned. (Point marked A on Plate VI.) A

week later the carefully built-up improvement in morale
had been dissipated and the pessimism had revived in full
force. This change was brought to the attention of management and the rest-periods were formally re-instituted.
(Plate VI, point B.) Unfortunately the unsatisfactory
plan of making the men "earn" their rests was also restored. In March, consequently, the incidence of rest-
periods was highly uncertain and irregular. On a given
day certain men might have no rests at all; others would
have one, two, three, or, rarely, four. In spite of this,
the chart shows distinct improvement in the later weeks
in March, an improvement which was reflected in a more
cheerful mental attitude.

At the end of March the performance of the group
showed itself as low—the monthly average had returned
to 70 per cent. The president of the Company called a
conference and at its conclusion ordered that, during the
month of April, the spinning mules should be shut down
four times a day for ten minutes at a time, and that all
hands from head-tenders to "piecers" should lie down and
rest as they had been instructed to do. Adequate floor
space and sufficient sacking for comfort created difficulties, because forty men had to lie down simultaneously
by their machines. This was contrived, however, and the
incidence of rest-periods arranged so that the first ten-
minute rest came after two hours' work, the second after
work for one hour and a half. This left a concluding work-
period in each spell of one hour and ten minutes. The
experiment was a success; the figures for April showed a
ten per cent improvement over March in spite of the fact
that the machines had been shut down while forty men
rested for forty minutes every day. In May the president
ordered a return to the method of alternating rest-

periods, one man at a time in each alley—the alley itself to determine the order of succession. In May the efficiency figure was 80¼, in June 85, July 82, and so on. For the sixteen months after April, 1924, the flat average was 83 per cent—the lowest 79½, the highest 86½. There were other changes of interest. For example, the months when production was highest—September and October, 1924, May and June, 1925—were months in which demand was urgent. The months when production was lower—December, 1924, January, 1925—were months in which work was slack and irregular. Before the innovation in method, the contrary was true. It was also noticed that Monday and Friday were no longer the worst days in the week; again, the performance of a given day tended to relate itself to the demand of that day. The irregularity of daily production observable in May (Plate VI, point C) was due to the fact that, working under the new conditions, the mules were constantly outrunning the carding machines which supplied them with yarn.

The original problem was to devise a method of diminishing a very high labor turnover. In the experimental twelve-month period there was no labor turnover at all. A few workers left the department, one because his family removed to the country, certain others were "laid off" in a slack period. But the problem of an emotional labor turnover ceased to exist. The factory held its workers and had no difficulty in maintaining a full complement even in times of rushed work. The president of the Company in a speech made some years later, claimed that, consequent on the innovation, the labor turnover in the spinning department had fallen from 250 per cent to the steady 5 per cent which was regarded as normal to the whole establishment.

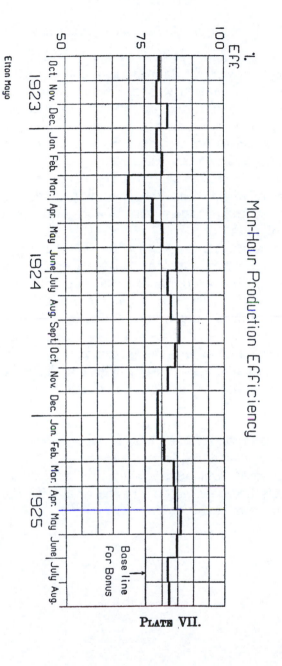

PRODUCTION – SPINNING MULES – TWENTY-THREE MONTHS

Man-Hour Production Efficiency

Plate VII.

Here, then, is an instance of the manner in which one industrial company worked its way through an acute human problem to a solution very much in accord with the principles later enunciated by Wyatt. At suitable intervals, change was introduced. Payment according to output was to some extent achieved by the consistent earning of bonuses. The work was broken up into self-contained tasks and ceased to be an interminable activity. The social inter-relations within the group improved both within the factory and outside it. Rests were introduced into the spell of work.

Monotony, like fatigue, is a word which is used to denote any sort of induced unbalance in the worker such that he cannot continue work, or can continue only at a lower level of activity. There are many possibilities of such unbalance—different individuals and different situations. Inquiry into such situations looks for some contributing factor or factors in external conditions, something also in the individual himself. The unbalance is, in Cannon's words, both interofective and exterofective; there is a disequilibrium within the individual and between him and his work. In the case cited, the complicating problem was that of the mental preoccupations—pessimism and rage—induced in the workers by the conditions of their work. But neither they nor their immediate supervisors had been able to define or specify the contributory external conditions.

CHAPTER III

THE HAWTHORNE EXPERIMENT. WESTERN ELECTRIC COMPANY

THAT conception of the conditions of biological experiment which I have quoted from L. J. Henderson and the Harvard Fatigue Laboratory, certain officers of the Western Electric Company had derived from experience. I do not mean that they had clearly stated or set down the special difficulties attendant upon biological inquiry as compared with chemical or physical analysis. At the time of which I speak, the year 1926, they had empirically discovered that one may organize, and apparently scientifically, a carefully contrived inquiry into a human industrial problem and yet fail completely to elucidate the problem in any particular. Acting in collaboration with the National Research Council, the Western Electric Company had for three years been engaged upon an attempt to assess the effect of illumination upon the worker and his work. No official report of these experiments has yet been published, and it is consequently impossible to quote chapter and verse as to the methods employed and the results obtained. I can, however, state with confidence that the inquiry involved in one phase the segregation of two groups of workers, engaged upon the same task, in two rooms equally illuminated. The experimental diminution of the lighting, in ordered quantities, in one room only, gave no sufficiently significant difference, expressed in terms of measured output, as compared with the other still fully illuminated room. Somehow or other that complex of mutually dependent factors, the human organism, shifted its equilibrium and unintentionally defeated the purpose of the experiment.

This interesting failure must be held in part responsible for the provocation to further experiment. But in addition to this problem of method, there were many concrete questions of high importance to which the executive authority desired objective answers, independent of executive opinion. Fatigue, monotony, and their effects upon work and worker were topics of much contemporary discussion. Was it possible to demonstrate clearly the part played by these in industrial situations? Furthermore, any company controlling many thousand workers tends naturally to develop its own methods or "policies," but tends also to lack any satisfactory criterion of the actual value of its methods of dealing with people. Whereas a machine will in some way reveal an inefficiency, a method of handling human situations will rarely reveal that it is rooted in mere custom and use rather than wisdom. These various considerations led to the institution of a second inquiry or series of inquiries in April, 1927.

In the institution of this second inquiry full heed was paid to the lesson of the first experiment. A group of workers was segregated for observation of the effect of various changes in the conditions of work. No attempt was made to "test for the effect of single variables." Where human beings are concerned one cannot change one condition without inadvertently changing others— so much the illumination experiment had shown. The group was kept small—six operatives—because the Company officers had become alert to the possible significance for the inquiry of changes of mental attitude; it was believed that such changes were more likely to be noticed by the official observers if the group were small. Arrangements were made to measure accurately all changes in output; this also meant that the group must be small. An accurate record of output was desired for two reasons: first, changes in production differ from many other human changes in that they lend themselves to exact and continuous determination; second, variations in output do effectively show "the combined effect" of all the conditions affecting a group. The work of Vernon and Wyatt supports the view than an output curve does indicate the relative equilibrium or disequilibrium of the individual and the group.

The operation selected was that of assembling telephone relays. This consists in "putting together a coil, armature, contact springs, and insulators in a fixture and securing the parts in position by means of four machine screws"; each assembly takes about one minute, when work is going well.[1] The operation ranks as repetitive; it is performed by women. A standard assembly bench with places for five workers and the appropriate equipment were put into one of the experimental rooms. This room was separated from the main assembly department by a ten-foot wooden partition. The bench was well illuminated; arrangements were made for observation of temperature and humidity changes. An attempt was made to provide for the observation of other changes and especially of unanticipated changes as well as those experimentally introduced. This again reflected the experience gained in the illumination experiments. Thus constituted, presumably for a relatively short period of ob-

[1] *Personnel Journal,* Vol. VIII, No. 5, p. 299.

servation, the experimental room actually ran on from April, 1927, to the middle of 1932, a period of over five years. And the increasing interest of the experiment justified its continuance until the economic depression made further development impossible.

Six female operatives were chosen, five to work at the bench, one to procure and distribute parts for those engaged in assembly. I shall not discuss the method of choosing these operatives, except to say that all were experienced workers. This was arranged by those in charge because they wished to avoid the complications which learning would introduce. Within the first year the two operatives first chosen—numbers one and two at the outset—dropped out, and their places were taken by two other workers of equal or superior skill who remained as numbers one and two until the end. The original number five left the Hawthorne Works for a time in the middle period but subsequently returned to her place in the group. In effect, then, there exist continuous records of the output of five workers for approximately five years. These records were obtained by means of a specially devised apparatus which, as each relay was completed, punched a hole in a moving tape. The tape moved at a constant speed, approximately one-quarter of an inch per minute; it punched five rows of holes, one row for each worker. At the right of each worker's place at the bench was a chute within which was an electric gate. When the worker finished a relay she placed it in the chute; as it passed through, it operated the electric gate and the punching apparatus duly recorded the relay. By measuring the distance on the tape between one hole and the next it is possible to calculate the time elapsing between the completion of one relay and another. The

Company thus has a record of every relay assembled by every operative in the experimental room for five years and in almost every instance has also a record of the time taken to assemble it. These exceptionally interesting figures are being analyzed by my colleague, T. N. Whitehead.

The transfer of the five workers into the experimental room was carefully arranged. It was clear that changes in output, as measured by the recording device, would constitute the most important series of observations. The continuity and accuracy of this record would obviously make it the chief point of reference for other observations. Consequently, for two weeks before the five operatives were moved into the special room, a record was kept of the production of each one without her knowledge. This is stated as the base output from which she starts. After this, the girls were moved into the experimental room and again for five weeks their output was recorded without the introduction of any change of working conditions or procedures. This, it was assumed, would sufficiently account for any changes incidental to the transfer. In the third period, which lasted for eight weeks, the experimental change introduced was a variation in method of payment. In the department the girls had been paid a group piece rate as members of a group of approximately one hundred workers. The change in the third period was to constitute the five a unitary group for piece-rate payment. "This meant that each girl would earn an amount more nearly in proportion to her individual effort since she was paid with a group of five instead of a group of one hundred." [2] It also meant that each girl was given a strong, though indirect, interest in the

[2] *Personnel Journal, loc. cit.,* p. 301.

achievement of the group. After watching the effect of this change of grouping for eight weeks, the Company officers felt that the more significant experimentation might begin.

In the fourth experimental period the group was given two rest-pauses of five minutes each, beginning at 10:00 in the mid-morning and at 2:00 in the afternoon respectively. The question had been discussed beforehand with the operatives—as all subsequent changes were—and the decision had been in favor of a five minute rather than a ten or fifteen minute pause partly because there was some feeling that, if the break were longer, the lost time would perhaps not be made up. This was continued for five weeks, at which time it was clear that just as total output [3] had increased perceptibly after the constitution of the workers as a group for payment, so also had it definitely risen again in response to the rests. The alternative of the original proposals, two ten-minute rest-pauses, was therefore adopted as the experimental change in period five. This change was retained for four weeks, in which time both the daily and weekly output of the group showed a greater rise than for any former change. In the sixth period the group was given six five-minute rests for four weeks. The girl operatives expressed some dislike of the constant interruption and the output curve showed a small recession.

The seventh experimental period was destined to become standard for the remaining years of the experiment.

[3] The output figures to which I refer here and in succeeding paragraphs are those figures which were made available in contemporary reports of the experiment. These figures are being carefully revised by T. N. Whitehead and his assistants and will be published in due course. I have no ground for assuming that the revision will make any essential difference in the facts described. And in any event it was upon the records I quote that the experimental development was based.

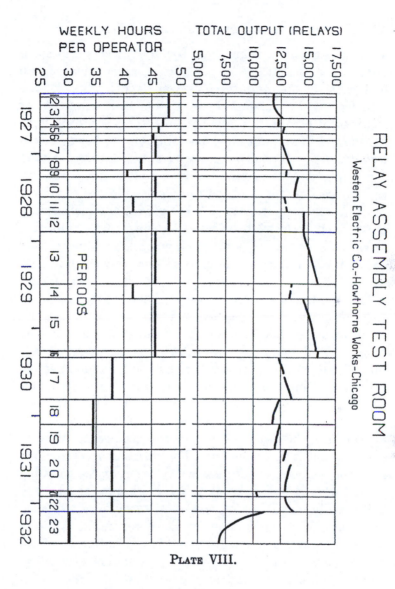

PLATE VIII.

The subsequent changes are, for the most part, some variation of it. It may be regarded as concluding the first phase of the inquiry which was devoted, first, to the transfer of the operative and the establishment of routines of observation and, second, to experiment with rest-pauses of varying incidence and length. Period seven was originally intended to discover the effect of giving some refreshment—coffee or soup and a sandwich—to the workers in the mid-morning period. The observers in charge had, in process of talking with the girls, found out that they frequently came to work in the morning after little or no breakfast. They became hungry long before lunch and it was thought that there was an indication of this in a downward trend of the output record before the midday break. It was therefore decided that the Company should supply each member of the group with adequate refection in the middle of the working morning and perhaps some slighter refreshment in the mid-afternoon. This, however, meant an abandonment of the six five-minute rests and a return to the two ten-minute rest-pauses. Such a return was in any event justified both by the expressed preference of the workers and by the fact that the output records seemed to indicate it as the better arrangement. The refreshment provided, however, made necessary some extension of the morning break. Period seven accordingly is characterized by a mid-morning break of fifteen minutes (9:30 A.M.) with lunch and a mid-afternoon break of ten minutes (2:30 P.M.). This arrangement persisted in uncomplicated form for eleven weeks and in that time production returned to its former high level and remained there.

In the second phase of experimentation, periods eight to eleven inclusive, the conditions of period seven are held constant and other changes are introduced. In period eight the group stopped work half an hour earlier every day—at 4:30 P.M. This was attended with a remarkable rise in both daily and weekly output. This continued for seven weeks until the tenth of March, 1928. Early in this period the original numbers one and two dropped out and their places were taken by those who rank as one and two for the greater part of the inquiry. In the ninth period the working day was shortened still further and the group stopped at 4:00 P.M. daily. This lasted for four weeks and in that time there was a slight fall both in daily and weekly output—although the average hourly output rose. In the tenth period the group returned to the conditions of work of period seven—fifteen-minute morning rest-pause with refreshment, ten-minute rest-pause in mid-afternoon and a full working day to five o'clock. This period lasted for twelve weeks and in that time the group in respect of its recorded daily and weekly output achieved and held a production very much higher than at any previous time. It was, perhaps, this "high" of production which brought to expression certain grave doubts which had been growing in the minds of the Company officers responsible for the experiment. Many changes other than those in production had been observed to be occurring; up to this time it had been possible to assume for practical purposes that such changes were of the nature of adaptation to special circumstance and not necessarily otherwise significant. Equally it had been possible to assume that the changes recorded in output were, at least for the most part, related to the experimental changes in working conditions—rest-pauses or whatnot—singly and successively imposed. At this stage these assumptions had become untenable—especially in the light of the previously expressed determination "not to test for single variables" but to study the situation.

Period eleven was a concession to the workers, at least in part. I do not mean that the Company had not intended to extend their second experimental phase—observation of the effect of shorter working time—to include a record of the effect of a five-day week. I am convinced that this was intended; but the introduction of a shorter working week—no work on Saturday—at this time refers itself to two facts, first, that the twelve weeks of this period run between the second of July and the first of September in the summer of 1928 and, second, it refers itself also by anticipation to the next experimental change. For it had already been agreed between the workers and the officers in charge that the next experiment, twelve, should be the restoration of the original conditions of work—no rest-pauses, no lunch, no shortened day or week. In period eleven—the shortened week in summer—the daily output continued to increase; it did not, however, increase sufficiently to compensate for the loss of Saturday morning's work, consequently the weekly output shows a small recession. It is important to note that although the weekly output shows this recession, it nevertheless remains above the weekly output of all other periods except periods eight and ten.

September, 1928, was an important month in the development of the inquiry. In September, the twelfth experimental change began and, by arrangement with the workers, continued for twelve weeks. In this period, as I have said, the group returned to the conditions of work which obtained in period three at the beginning of the inquiry; rest-periods, special refreshments, and other concessions were all abolished for approximately three months. In September, 1928, also began that extension of the inquiry known as "The Interview Programme" which I shall discuss in the next chapter. Both of these events must be regarded as having strongly influenced the course of the inquiry.

The history of the twelve-week return to the so-called original conditions of work is soon told. The daily and weekly output rose to a point higher than at any other time and in the whole period "there was no downward trend." At the end of twelve weeks, in period thirteen, the group returned, as had been arranged, to the conditions of period seven with the sole difference that whereas the Company continued to supply coffee or other beverage for the mid-morning lunch, the girls now provided their own food. This arrangement lasted for thirty-one weeks—much longer than any previous change. Whereas in period twelve the group's output had exceeded that of all the other performances, in period thirteen, with rest-pauses and refreshment restored, their output rose once again to even greater heights. It had become clear that the itemized changes experimentally imposed, although they could perhaps be used to account for minor differences between one period and another, yet could not be used to explain the major change—the continually increasing production. This steady increase as represented by all the contemporary records seemed to ignore the experimental changes in its upward development.

The fourteenth experimental period was a repetition of period eleven; it permitted the group to give up work on Saturday between the first of July and the thirty-first of August, 1929. The fifteenth period returned again to the conditions of the thirteenth, and at this point we may regard the conditions of period seven as the established standard for the group.

It had been the habit of the officers in charge to issue reports of the progress of the experiment from time to time. These reports were published privately to the Western Electric Company and certain of its officers. From these documents one can gain some idea of the contemporary attitude to the inquiry of those who were directing it. The third of these reports was issued on August 15, 1928, and consequently did not carry its comment or description beyond period ten. The fourth was issued on May 11, 1929, and in it one finds interesting discussion of the events I have just described. The first allusion to the problem is a remark to the effect that "although periods seven, ten, and thirteen involve the same length working day, the upward trend has continued through all three of these periods" (p. 34). Later the report says: "The increased production during the test has taken the operators from an average weekly output of about 2,400 relays (each) at the beginning to a present average weekly output of about 3,000 relays. (Period 13, which lasted until the end of June, 1929.) Periods seven, ten, and thirteen had the same working conditions; namely, a fifteen-minute rest and lunch in the morning and a ten-minute rest in the afternoon. Yet the average weekly output for the group in period seven was a little over 2,500 relays each, for period ten it was a little over 2,800 relays, and for period thirteen it was about 3,000 relays. Furthermore, period twelve was like period three in working conditions requiring a full day's work without any lunch or rest. Yet the average output for period three was less than 2,500 relays a week and that for period twelve was more than 2,900 relays a week.

Period twelve was continued for twelve weeks and there was no downward trend. . . . The hourly output rate was distinctly higher during the full working day of period twelve than during the full working day of period three. Between the comparable periods seven, ten, and thirteen the rate of production also increased" (p. 84).

As instances of the "outcome" of the experiment the report mentions the interviewing programme, also the fact that the rest-pause system had been extended to about 3,000 employees in various departments (p. 125). From the "conclusions" I select the following passages:

"(b) There has been a continual upward trend in output which has been independent of the changes in rest-pauses. This upward trend has continued too long to be ascribed to an initial stimulus from the novelty of starting a special study."

"(c) The reduction of muscular fatigue has not been the primary factor in increasing output. Cumulative fatigue is not present."

"(f) There has been an important increase in contentment among the girls working under test-room conditions."

"(g) There has been a decrease in absences of about 80 per cent among the girls since entering the test-room group. Test-room operators have had approximately one-third as many sick absences as the regular department during the last six months" (p. 126).

"(v) Output is more directly related to the type of working day than to the number of (working) days in the week . . ." (p. 127).

"(y) Observations of operators in the relay assembly test room indicate that their health is being maintained

RELAY ASSEMBLY TEST ROOM

Western Electric Co.-Hawthorne Works-Chicago

Average Hourly Output-Smoothed Curves

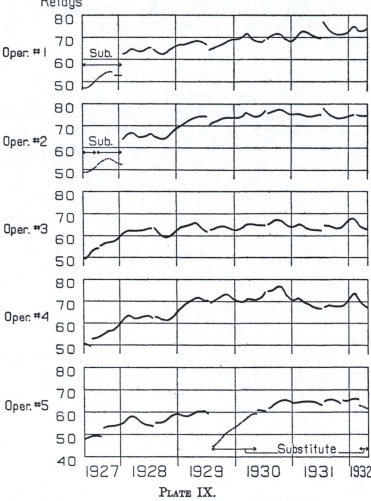

PLATE IX.

or improved and that they are working within their capacity . . ." (p. 129).

The following conclusions in former reports are re-affirmed:

"(n) The changed working conditions have resulted in creating an eagerness on the part of operators to come to work in the morning" (p. 130).

"(s) Important factors in the production of a better mental attitude and greater enjoyment of work have been the greater freedom, less strict supervision and the opportunity to vary from a fixed pace without reprimand from a gang boss."

"The operators have no clear idea as to why they are able to produce more in the test room; but as shown in the replies to questionnaires . . . there is the feeling that better output is in some way related to the distinctly pleasanter, freer, and happier working conditions" (p. 131).

The report proceeds to remark that "much can be gained industrially by carrying greater personal consideration to the lowest levels of employment."

Mr. G. A. Pennock in a paper read before a conference of the Personnel Research Federation on September 15, 1929, in New York says: ". . . this unexpected and continual upward trend in productivity throughout the periods, even in period twelve when the girls were put on a full forty-eight hour week with no rest period or lunch, led us to seek some explanation or analysis." He goes on to mention three possibilities: first, fatigue which he finds it easy to exclude on the medical evidence, on the basis of certain physiological findings, and on the obvious ground that the "gradually rising production over a period of two years" precludes such a possibility.

He considers that the payment incentive of the higher group earnings may play some small part, but proceeds to state his conviction that the results are mainly due to changes in mental attitude. He proceeds to cite evidence to show the extent of this change.

It will be remembered that one of the avowed intentions of this inquiry was to observe as well as might be the unanticipated changes, including changes of mental attitude. The method overtly adopted at the beginning of the inquiry is stated in an early report as follows:

"C. *Pertinent Records*

Other records pertinent to the test and of value as an aid in interpreting results and psychological effects are maintained as follows:

1. The temperature and relative humidity, which are recorded each hour and then averaged, are plotted on the daily average hourly curve.

2. A complete report of the daily happenings (history sheets) of the test is made and this records what changes are made; what transpires during the day; operators' remarks; our own observations; and anything that will assist as an explanation when rationalizing the performance curve.

3. A "Log Sheet" is maintained on each operator upon which her starting and finishing time is entered, and the time at which changes from one type to another are made; also all intervals, or non-productive time, such as personal time out, changes in type, repairs, and anything detracting from the actual production time.

4. An original hospital report, or record of physical examination, is kept. This has been supplemented each time the group is reëxamined which occurs periodically every five or six weeks. . . .

5. An attempt was made to discover the home and social environs of each girl worker. . . .

6. Data have been gathered in the attempt to reflect what in the judgment of the operators themselves is the reason why they do better work under test-room conditions. . . ." [4]

These original provisions were effective largely because the experimental room was in charge of an interested and sympathetic chief observer. He understood clearly from the first that any hint of "the supervisor" in his methods might be fatal to the interests of the inquiry. So far as it was possible he and his assistants kept the history sheets and the log sheet faithfully posted. In addition to this he took a personal interest in each girl and her achievement; he showed pride in the record of the group. He helped the group to feel that its duty was to set its own conditions of work, he helped the workers to find the "freedom" of which they so frequently speak.

In the early stages of development, it was inevitable that the group should become interested in its achievement and should to some extent enjoy the reflected glory of the interest the inquiry attracted. As the years passed this abated somewhat, but all the evidence—including the maintenance of a high output—goes to show that something in the reconditioning of the group must be regarded as a permanent achievement. At no time in the five-year period did the girls feel that they were working under pressure; on the contrary they invariably cite the absence of this as their reason for preferring the "test room."

The reason, then, for Mr. Pennock's claim is plain. Undoubtedly, there had been a remarkable change of mental attitude in the group. This showed in their recurrent conferences with high executive authorities. At first shy and uneasy, silent and perhaps somewhat suspicious

[4] Third Report, Western Electric Company, pp. 2, 3.

of the Company's intention, later their attitude is marked by confidence and candor. Before every change of programme, the group is consulted. Their comments are listened to and discussed; sometimes their objections are allowed to negative a suggestion. The group unquestionably develops a sense of participation in the critical determinations and becomes something of a social unit. This developing social unity is illustrated by the entertainment of each other in their respective homes, especially operatives one, two, three, and four.

How can a change such as this be assessed? It is a change of mental attitude; it is also far more. There is no possibility of comparison with those industrial situations in which Vernon or Wyatt or some other investigator for the Fatigue Board is given authority to interpolate rest-pauses. In any such instance, the institution of rest-pauses is probably the only major change and it takes time, as Vernon has pointed out, for those secondary changes to be effected which finally show in increased output—amongst other effects. By "secondary changes" I mean those secondary effects of rest-pauses such as diminished discontent with work and working conditions and all that may imply in human thought.

There is not even any great likeness between the rest-pauses instituted in the Philadelphia textile mill and the Western Electric experiment. There is, perhaps, some slight resemblance in that the benefit of the rest-pauses in the spinning department was much supplemented by the skilled interviewing of the investigating nurse. An additional resemblance, though again slight, is perhaps to be found in the dramatic intervention of the Company president in favor of the workers at a critical moment in the inquiry. But once again it must be affirmed that no identity can be found as between these situations.

The most significant change that the Western Electric Company introduced into its "test room" bore only a casual relation to the experimental changes. What the Company actually did for the group was to reconstruct entirely its whole industrial situation. Miss May Smith has wisely observed that the repetition work is "a thread of the total pattern," but "is not the total pattern." The Company, in the interest of developing a new form of scientific control—namely, measurement and accurate observation—incidentally altered the total pattern, in Miss Smith's analogy, and then experimented with that thread which, in this instance, was the work of assembling relays. The consequence was that there was a period during which the individual workers and the group had to re-adapt themselves to a new industrial milieu, a milieu in which their own self-determination and their social well-being ranked first and the work was incidental. The experimental changes—rest-pauses, food, and talk at appropriate intervals—perhaps operated at first mainly to convince them of the major change and to assist the readaptation. But once the new orientation had been established, it became proof against the minor experimental changes. At Hawthorne as the situation developed the experimental changes became minor matters in actuality —whatever the operatives thought. In Vernon's work, in Wyatt's, and at Philadelphia the equivalent changes were not minor but were rather developments upon which the whole success of a new plan depended. Not so at Hawthorne: with respect to period twelve any theory that there was "a return to original conditions" is nonsensical. At that time the new industrial milieu, the new "total pattern," had been sufficiently established and the repetition work, "the thread," ran true to this, its chief determinant.

It must not be supposed that the abandonment of rest-pauses and other concessions in period twelve was without effect. On the contrary the "personal time out" reverted to its original dimension; in none of the periods between twelve and three does it bulk as large as in twelve and three. The average hourly output was stated at the time to have diminished. But these minor consequences were obscured by the major achievement, the capacity of the group—unsuspected even by themselves —to ignore an interference and continue their response to the major change—the novel industrial milieu. All this is, of course, mere description of an empirical kind antecedent to analysis. The analysis proceeds and will at some later time be reported. In the meantime it is of interest to observe the manner in which the Western Electric experiment echoes the biological findings of Cyril Burt and May Smith, of L. J. Henderson and his colleagues of the Fatigue Laboratory. May Smith quotes Cyril Burt's apt description of "multiple determination" in his discussion of juvenile delinquency. "A particular result is not caused by some one factor operating equally on all people, so that the presence of this factor invariably would produce the same results. Rather is it that there are several factors which together, operating on a particular temperament, will produce the result." The Fatigue Laboratory researches show us a number of mutually dependent factors in equilibrium, a change in external conditioning, and a change throughout the whole organization which is the organism. In the presence of such a change the individual may be able, by virtue of a shift of inner equilibrium, to keep going without effort or damage; the diagram which showed the difference between the athlete and untrained persons illustrated this. Or the inner equilibrium may be temporarily overthrown, in which case the untrained man stops running. The athlete can achieve a "steady state" in a greater variety of external changes and under conditions demanding much greater effort—having achieved this adjustment of inner equilibrium he "keeps going indefinitely." The Western Electric experiment was primarily directed not to the external condition but to the inner organization. By strengthening the "temperamental" inner equilibrium of the workers, the Company enabled them to achieve a mental "steady state" which offered a high resistance to a variety of external conditions.

I have said that this is merely descriptive and is no more than a first step towards the requisite analysis. T. N. Whitehead, by a fortunate use of mathematics, has embarked upon an analysis of the records of output which promises to be of the highest interest. I cannot present his work, nor shall I attempt to anticipate his illuminating findings. I shall merely indicate one or two of the directions in which his work is leading—this by way of arousing some alertness to what is to come. For example, he tends to the view that learning and skill are not capacities which are achieved once and for all time by a given individual. On the contrary the individual's skill is re-achieved each day and consequently depends in some degree upon the external conditions of that day and inner equilibrium. While this would probably be admitted at once by any neurologist, its demonstration from a work-curve is unusual. He finds also that in a group such as that described the determination of muscular movement is partly socially and partly individually conditioned. The gross muscular movements seem to be determined by one's neighbors after some years of association; the manipulative movements appear to be more individual. This has an effect both on output and on accidents because both are products of the relation between the speed and dexterity of gross muscular and of manipulative movement.

In my next chapter I turn to the analyses of their experimental findings attempted by the Western Electric Company.

CHAPTER IV

DEVELOPMENT OF THE WESTERN ELECTRIC INQUIRY. THE INTERVIEW PROGRAM

MR. M. L. PUTNAM of the Western Electric Company in a paper read before the Personnel Research Federation in New York on November 15, 1929, said: "The records of the test room [see Chap. III] showed a continual improvement in the performance of the operators regardless of the (experimental) changes made during the study. It was also noticed . . . that there was a marked improvement in their attitude toward their work and working environment. This simultaneous improvement in attitude and effectiveness indicated that there might be a definite relationship between them. In other words, we could more logically attribute the increase in efficiency to a betterment of morale than to any of the . . . alterations made in the course of the experiment. We concluded that the same relationship might exist throughout the plant and that the best way to improve morale . . . was through improved supervision." [1] Speaking at the same meeting, Mr. G. A. Pennock said: "A relationship of confidence and friendliness has been established with these girls to such an extent that practically no supervision is required. In the absence of any drive or urge whatsoever they can be depended upon to do their best. They say they have no sensation of working faster now than under the previous conditions. . . .

[1] *Personnel Journal*, Vol. VIII, No. 5, Feb., 1930, p. 315.

Comment after comment from the girls indicates that they have been relieved of the nervous tension under which they previously worked. They have ceased to regard the man in charge as a 'boss' . . . they have a feeling that their increased production is in some way related to the distinctly freer, happier, and more pleasant working environment." [*]

I have quoted from these two papers rather than from the contemporary report because the quotations state directly the ideas which were then preoccupying the minds of the officers in charge of the experiment. The improvement in production, they believe, is not very directly related to the rest-pauses and other innovations. It reflects rather a freer and more pleasant working environment, a supervisor who is not regarded as a "boss," a "higher morale." In this situation the production of the group insensibly lifts, even though the girls are not aware that they are working faster. Many times over, the history sheets and other records show that in the opinion of the group all supervision has been removed. On occasion indeed they artlessly tell the observer, who is in fact of supervisory rank, very revealing tales of their experiences with previous "bosses." Their opinion is, of course, mistaken: in a sense they are getting closer supervision than ever before, the change is in the quality of the supervision. This—the change in quality of supervision—is by no means the whole change, but it is an important part of it. Two questions, therefore, propose themselves to the directors of the inquiry. The first is a question as to the actual quality of the supervision outside the experimental room and in the plant. The second is a question as to the nature of an ordinary working

[*] *Loc. cit.*, p. 309.

environment from a worker's point of view. Is it so little free and happy as the development of the test room seems to suggest? Almost simultaneously, therefore, the Industrial Research Division embarks upon two inquiries designed to develop further these questions. These two inquiries are the "mica-room" experiment, begun in August, 1928, and the interviewing program, which was instituted in September of the same year.

The mica-room experiment was simply designed to repeat the essential features of the relay-assembly inquiry in order to see whether the same results would follow. "The work of a mica splitter is to separate thick sheets of mica into thin sheets of standard thickness (a few thousandths of an inch) with a pointed instrument. Each thin sheet is then tested in automatic calipers to determine whether it is within the limits of thickness allowed. . . . This work requires precise movements and close attention . . . the expertness and output of an operator increase appreciably over the first two or three years of work on this job."

"The output of five experienced operators was determined over a period of eight weeks beginning August 27, 1928. During this time the girls were working in the regular department and did not know that output records were being taken or that any special attention was being paid to their production."

"On October 22, 1928, the five operators were moved to a small test room, well lighted . . . partly partitioned off from one of the regular departments. The plan . . . was to try the effect of rest-pauses. This was explained. . . . They were willing to enter upon the study and were interested in it. . . ." [*]

[*] Fourth Report, Western Electric Company, May, 1929, p. 104.

For five weeks after removal to their new quarters, the group worked under the same conditions as before without experimental change. This was a repetition of the procedure adopted in the original experiment. Thereafter they were given two ten-minute rest-periods, at 9:30 A.M. and at 2:30 P.M., until the conclusion of the test. The reason assigned at the time for not introducing changes in respect to the incidence and length of rest-periods was that the experience with the original test room had shown that the "upward trend . . . was independent of the number and length of rest-pauses."

The general conditions for this experiment were in part determined by factors in the situation outside the control of the Industrial Research Division. The operatives had been working overtime for some time previous to the institution of the test. These conditions—a six-day week of fifty-five and one-half hours—lasted through the first period of eight weeks in the regular department, the second period of five weeks in their new quarters and for approximately thirty weeks of the third period, the period, namely, in which rest-pauses were instituted. After this, from June 15, 1929, comes a fourth period in which the operatives return to a normal week of forty-eight hours, the rest-period arrangement persisting. This continues for nearly a year until May 19, 1930, when, owing to the economic depression, their week is shortened to forty hours. This lasted for about four months, when the study was abandoned.

In spite of the overtime complication, the results of the original relay-assembly study were in some degree confirmed. After the institution of rest-periods the average hourly output is maintained and perhaps increased. This increase is quickened and reaches its maximum in what I have called the fourth period—when the girls were working a normal day with no overtime and with two ten-minute rests. This experiment was, however, no more than the first, a clear demonstration of the effect of rest-periods. When the group was moved into the experimental room they came automatically under the charge of the Industrial Research Division and especially under the supervision of the observer who had from the first arranged the various procedures of the original experiment. Here once again, therefore, one is forced to the conclusion that the rest-pause innovations are part of, and subsidiary to, a more extensive change of industrial milieu. At a much later period of the research a skilled investigator of the division reported some interviews with the girls of the original "test room." In this report she remarks that, on the basis of comments made by these operatives to her, their preference for the atmosphere of the experimental room seems mainly based on "the absence of objectionable administrative and supervisory practices" of which formerly they had experience. The differences seem to state themselves thus, in the opinion of the operatives concerned:

"In the test room there is:

    a. No interruption to flow of work.
    b. No "bogey" to work up to.
    c. No "boss" or slave-driving.
    d. No "stalling" (*i.e.* restriction).
    e. No insistence upon picking up dropped
       parts, etc."

It must not be assumed that these were actually the leading characteristics of work at Hawthorne. On the contrary, working conditions there have long been admitted by workers generally to be very superior to those which obtain elsewhere. This is simply a type of statement almost inevitably made when a not very articulate group of workers tries to express an indefinable feeling of relief from constraint. There can be no question that the mica workers also experienced this relief.

The mica study was designed to be confirmatory of the original study; the interviewing programme was an attempt to extend the investigation, and by a different method. It had become clear that there was a profound difference between the general conditions of work—socially and personally considered—in the two test rooms and in the regular departments. This difference seemed to relate itself to something in the quality of the supervision and to something experienced as an irksome constraint—in other words, to relate itself to the two questions specified above. The latter of these two questions was perhaps not fully explicit at this time, the former, namely, that as to current methods of supervision, was expressly stated in the earliest drafts of the programme. A contemporary statement in an official document reads: "It was thought that if all employees could be interviewed and their honest comments secured, they would give a comprehensive picture of the supervisory practices followed and of the desirability of these practices." [4] A statement of the "purpose of the programme" follows:

"1. To learn from employees their likes and dislikes relative to their working status.

"2. To provide a more definite and reliable basis for supervisory training and for added . . . control of proper working conditions, placement, and efficiency.

"3. To supplement and verify conclusions reached

[4] Employee Interviewing Programme. W. E. Co., Sept. 1928, to Feb., 1929, p. 1.

from the test studies now being conducted with small operating groups."

It was decided to attempt the development of such a programme, and to begin by trying it "experimentally in our Inspection Organization which contained about sixteen hundred skilled and unskilled employees, with both shop and office workers represented. All of these employees were to be interviewed, so that a fair picture would be obtained of the things people in various types of work like and dislike." [5] Naturally the plans for such a project had to be carefully prepared. "All the supervisors in the organization (*i.e.* in the Inspection Branch) were called together and the plan was explained to them. Their criticism was invited and various points in the plan were discussed. Generally, the plan was subscribed to; only a few of the supervisors were doubtful. Five interviewers were selected from the supervisory group to secure comments from employees. Women were selected to interview women and men to interview men. The interviewers were instructed not to interview employees whom they knew, since acquaintanceship might influence the comments. All comments were to be kept confidential; names or reference numbers were not to be attached to the interviews, and any identifying statements which might reveal the employee or his location were not to be recorded. In order to avoid undue curiosity . . . only a few employees from one location were interviewed in the same day. When the employee was asked to comment, he was assured that he was invited and not ordered to express himself; for it was felt that voluntary comments would be most reliable." [6]

[5] Putnam, *Personnel Journal, loc. cit.,* p. 316.
[6] *Loc. cit.,* p. 316.

A much later report issued by the Industrial Research Division (in January, 1931) thus summarizes the events that followed the inauguration of the interviewing programme: "Following these general plans, the interviewing of the Inspection organization employees was begun in September, 1928, and completed early in 1929. These early interviews contained a wealth of material applicable to the objectives of the study. While the comments of employees were generally brief (the average interviewing time being thirty minutes per individual) the thoughts they expressed corroborated in many respects the test-room findings." [7] In addition to this, however, much was learned about the working situation "including employee attitudes and feelings to it." The interviews also provided material for discussion at supervisory conferences superior to any material previously used for training purposes (*i.e.* the training of supervisors). It was found that simultaneously with the beginning of the interviews, supervision improved. "This was unexpected," says the report, "but was understood as implying that supervisors were stimulated to improvement by the new interest in supervisory method." Very soon after the actual work had commenced, it became evident that "employees enjoyed the opportunity of expressing their thoughts." Requests for interviews were received, some requests coming from the supervisors themselves. It was accordingly determined to extend the interviews to group and section chiefs, namely to those in immediate charge of the rank and file. The supervisors interviewed were asked as to their opinion of the plan and its effect—this question being additional to the interview. "They reported very favorably about the plan; felt that it had not been

[7] Divisional Report, Jan., 1931, Section II, pp. 3 and 4.

embarrassing to them in any way; said that in their opinion employees were in favor of it; and were practically unanimous that it should be kept up and extended to other organizations in the Works." [8]

For the moment I shall postpone consideration of the type of comment made in interviews and its effect upon the development of the inquiry and shall instead sketch briefly the extension of the programme. Early in 1929 it was decided to interview another organization in the Works, that known as the Operating Branch, and to offer the supervisory training conferences to supervisors in that organization. "It was at this time that the Industrial Research Division was organized with functions then stated as follows:

1. To interview annually all employees to find out their likes and dislikes relative to their working status.

2. To study the favorable and unfavorable comments of employees.

    a. To initiate correction . . . of unfavorable comments (*i.e.* of problems indicated by unfavorable comments).

    b. To determine upon benefits . . . from favorable comments and . . . ways and means of acquiring these benefits.

3. To conduct supervisory training conferences for all supervisors—using employee interviews as basis.

4. To conduct test studies relative to employee relations, fatigue and efficiency." [9]

The plan for 1929 was to interview all the employees in the Operating Branch and to re-interview all the Inspec-

[8] *Ibid.*   [9] Report of the Division, Jan., 1931, Section II, p. 5.

tion Branch workers. This proved to be impossible because of the increasing time taken by each interview. It was nevertheless determined to extend the inquiry to all the organizations at Hawthorne and in January, 1930, this was put into effect. These successive extensions necessitated a considerable increase of staff, especially since the interviews were lengthening very considerably as the method of interviewing improved. "Employees assigned to interviewing . . . were usually supervisors; they were taken for a temporary period (full time) of about one year. It was felt not only that they could do the interviewing with proper training, but that the interviewing experience was in itself a training for them as supervisors. . . . In addition to this temporary personnel, a nucleus staff of permanent people was built up to take over some of the more technical aspects of the work. In 1929 forty-three people were trained in interviewing. In 1930 twenty replacements were made, only two of which were added to the permanent staff." [10] The approximate number engaged in interviewing in 1929 and 1930 was thirty.

The extension of the interview system is shown in the following table:

Branch	1928	1929	1930	Total
Inspection	1,600		514	2,114
Operating		10,300	5,109	15,409
Public Relations			8	8
Industrial Relations			130	130
Accounting			637	637
Production			963	963
Technical			1,166	1,166
Specialty Products			699	699
	1,600	10,300	9,226	21,126

In rather more than two years over twenty-one thousand employees, out of a total at that time of approximately

[10] *Ibid.,* p. 6.

forty thousand, were personally interviewed. In the earliest year the length of time occupied by the average interview was about thirty minutes; as the method developed and the confidence of employees increased the average interview came to take about one and one-half hours.

This brief description will suffice to give some idea of the extreme rapidity with which the interview project developed; it does not, however, show the changes of conception and method which this rapid development brought in its train. In origin the scheme was fairly clear. Two groups of operatives, selected to work in experimental rooms numbers one and two, had been chosen from departments where methods of supervision and conditions of work conformed to the high standards of the Company. The choice, especially in the first instance, relay assembling, was based upon the nature of the work as suited to the type of experiment and bore no reference to supervision and working conditions. The outcome of both experiments was such that inevitably questions suggested themselves as to whether industry really knew anything whatever about appropriate working conditions or proper supervisory methods. Interviewing in the first instance was accordingly designed to discover something in fact about supervision and working conditions and especially what workers liked or disliked in their work, in the conditions of work, and in supervisory method. Obviously some answers would be true and some false; but out of the welter of information some findings of value on which to base action might emerge. I do not mean to imply that anyone concerned in the inquiry ever stated or thought of the project quite as simply as my statement might seem to suggest. But I do not believe that anyone clearly anticipated the event.

That the difficulties were not underestimated is shown by the method adopted in the first interviews. Interviewers took with them mentally a questionnaire as to the likes and dislikes of the individual for his work, the conditions of his work, and supervision. This in a sense seems capable of simple reduction to six questions. But their instruction from the first was to avoid plumping six questions directly at the worker; they were told rather to engage him in conversation and to lead the conversation to the appropriate topics. Before the inquiry had been established for more than a month or two, one of the chief interests of the investigating group had become the all-absorbing topic—the proper method of conducting an interview. In some of the early interviews, the worker would talk for the time allotted but subsequent consideration of what he said would seem to show that he had answered none of the questions effectively. If the interviewer "adroitly led him back to the point in question" often "the employee would again revert to the subject of his own choosing." If this was not permitted there was danger of, in effect, putting an end to the interview. "It became obvious to the interviewers that, whatever the question, the thoughts of some employees tended to gravitate toward a particular condition or subject; that in these cases something was uppermost in the mind of the employee which completely overshadowed everything else. Cases were found where several subjects predominated . . . and any attempt to lead him away from his line of thought was generally unsuccessful. In other instances the interviewers found that a particularly taciturn person became remarkably communicative if just the right spot could be touched in conversation." [11] The

[11] Divisional Report, Jan., 1931, Section II, p. 9.

effect of these experiences was to provoke a doubt in the division. Did not these heavy preoccupations, these un-expected breaks into loquacity, indicate "a latent source of information" which the "early interviewing technique normally failed to tap?" [12] So attention was concentrated upon interviewing method and an improved method of interviewing was developed. The innovation echoes a finding reported by Smith and Culpin (quoted above, Chap. II) in their investigation of telegraphists' cramp: "It often happened that when once started the subject would give a very detailed personal account of himself, in which case the investigator would not interfere with questions." [13] The discovery at Hawthorne, made inde-pendently, is entirely confirmatory of all that Smith and Culpin claim. The divisional description of the innova-tion acknowledges its debt to Asclepias: "the technique now employed owes something to the methods developed by psychopathology; but it nevertheless differs in essen-tial respects, and is an industrial adaptation for use in normal human situations. Very briefly stated, the present method may be outlined as follows: the interviewer is introduced to the employee, and the interviewer 'catches on' in a conversational way at any starting point men-tioned by the employee. As long as an employee talks the interviewer follows his comments, displaying a real interest in what the employee has to say and taking suffi-cient notes to enable him to recall the employee's com-ments. While the employee continues, no attempt is made on the part of the interviewer to change the subject be-cause it is a basic assumption of the method that, where the employee chooses his own topics, he chooses them partly in their order of importance for him. If the inter-

[12] *Ibid.*   [13] I. F. R. B., No. 43, 1927, p. 16.

viewer were to ask questions or to redirect the employee's comment to other topics or subjects, he would in a sense ask the employee to talk upon a subject . . . not necessarily at all important to the employee. The interviewer takes part in the conversation only in so far as it is necessary to keep the employee talking and to stimulate confidence."

The report goes on to describe refinements of this method used by the more experienced and more skilled interviewers. The more skilled the conduct of an interview, the better its effect upon the employee. He not only says more and of more intimate topics but in the process of talking he discovers new interpretations for himself. "It is interesting, even if it cannot be fully explained, that such a procedure seems to lead to a change of attitude in the employee." The report cites here an interview with an employee who was described privately by her supervisor as a problem case. In the course of the interview—which occupies twenty pages of report—she makes the discovery that she dislikes this same supervisor merely on the ground of a fancied resemblance to a hated relative. This type of benefit differs from the mere "emotional release" afforded by expression in a simpler interview; it involves a personal achievement of a new attitude.

This statement serves to show the difficulties that emerged to complicate the inquiry. The more obvious type of interview that is content with possibly perfunctory answers to stated questions had been repudiated. Interviewers had been instructed to take real interest in what was said, whatever the topic. Staff discussion had shown them how interruption or impatience may serve to shatter a series of ideas struggling towards expression in a not very articulate person. They had been trained never to offer advice or help on the ground that any such procedure would immediately distort and change the relation between interviewer and person interviewed. Finally they had been told to gain in every interview from the person talking as clear an idea as possible of:

a. What he wants to say.
b. What he does not want to say.
c. What he cannot say without help.

The group of interviewers who actually did the work of 1929 and 1930 cannot be assumed to be as entirely inexperienced as the mere circumstance of their selection might suggest. Some could claim extensive experience of personnel work of various kinds, the majority had some years of service with the Company, a few unquestionably had a special capacity for this type of investigation. Considered as a group, they did their work very well—and were distinctly embarrassed by the result. In effect, the abandonment of the trivial interview and the adoption of the innovations in technique described above had served to provoke in even the most unlikely individuals that were interviewed a high confidence and an intimate personal revelation of attitude that was most difficult to assess. The practical consequence of such interviewing was generally admirable; both supervisors and employees displayed enthusiasm. "This is the best thing the Company ever did" or "the Company ought to have done this long ago" were expressions that were frequently encountered. The interviewing plan, in other words, would have been a sufficient success if it had merely been continued as a working plan to ease the human inter-relationships amongst a large and heterogeneous group of workers.

But this was not enough either for the research division or for the Company. The quest was for knowledge of what constituted good supervision and good working conditions; this knowledge was still remote.

The investigators themselves were nevertheless acquiring wisdom. They had learned that opinions are not detachable. What a worker thinks on a given subject is a symptom of what he is; his ideas cannot be torn out of their personal context and exhibited as significant. An interview that occupies nearly two hours and is largely made up of confidences as to personal history and personal experience gives an observer some insight into the significance for the individual of his experiences and beliefs. But it yields little that affords management a secure basis for executive action. Further, the more intimate the interview, the more difficult is it to analyze its content in such a fashion that it may be related to other interviews. It had been easy to include in the plan of the research division a department which should analyze interviews and discover their significant content. It was exceedingly difficult to devise methods by which this might in fact be accomplished.

This problem of interview analysis demands more explicit statement because the whole significance of the developing research is implicit in it. Generally speaking, actions or statements which express an articulate logic or a special skill are valid for other people in the relevant external context. Other actions or statements express a personal context and are little likely to be valid or even to possess meaning for other people or in any external context. It is profoundly true that the industrial executive needs to be trained in methods of understanding men and of controlling these all-too-human situations.

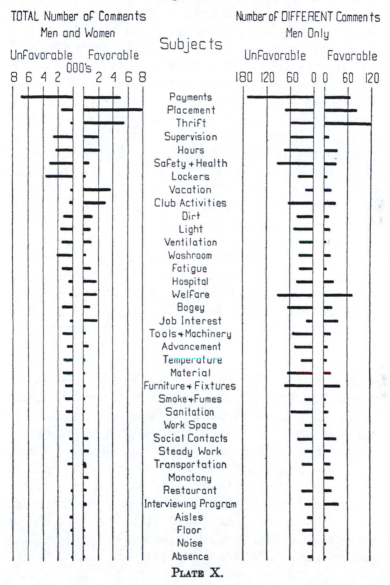

WESTERN ELECTRIC COMPANY
Operating Branch - 1929

TOTAL Number of Comments
Men and Women

Unfavorable   Favorable
000's
8 6 4 2   2 4 6 8

Subjects

Number of DIFFERENT Comments
Men Only

Unfavorable   Favorable
180 120 60 0   0 60 120

Payments
Placement
Thrift
Supervision
Hours
Safety + Health
Lockers
Vacation
Club Activities
Dirt
Light
Ventilation
Washroom
Fatigue
Hospital
Welfare
Bogey
Job Interest
Tools + Machinery
Advancement
Temperature
Material
Furniture + Fixtures
Smoke + Fumes
Sanitation
Work Space
Social Contacts
Steady Work
Transportation
Monotony
Restaurant
Interviewing Program
Aisles
Floor
Noise
Absence

PLATE X.

But at present, unfortunately, we have no developed method of simple expression for those statements which imply nothing objective beyond a personal attitude and a personal history. The problem for the interviewer and for the would-be analyst of interviews was that although the division was nominally seeking criticisms of Company policy that referred themselves to a reasoned and articulate logic of industrial organization, the whole method of inquiry committed them to the discovery of opinions that referred themselves to highly individual and personal experiences and situations. Moreover, this was the only kind of interviewing that was of any use. Employees wanted it; it eased their minds, it helped them to revise their too-personal opinions. The research division wanted it, because the division realized that the whole obscure problem of human inter-relation in an industrial organization was concealed somewhere in the dark area. Any less courageous diversion to other aims would be an evasion of the real issue.

Here, for example, is a diagram which represents an early attempt to analyze or to present in graphic form the content of the interviews recorded in the Operating Branch in 1929. You will recollect that, on account of the method employed, the topics listed represent subjects voluntarily chosen for discussion by employees. A selection has been made from ten thousand interviews of those topics, having some industrial reference, which were most frequently named. The diagram on the left shows the total of such comments classified as favorable or unfavorable to existing Company practice. The total comments on all subjects are said approximately to balance. The diagram on the right is designed to show the number of different ideas expressed. That is to say, the diagram on the right is what remains if, for any given topic, the "analyst" cancels out repetitions so that each critical or favorable idea appears only once. You will observe that this leaves, not for every topic but over all, a heavy balance of "unfavorable." This may not mean very much; it means at least that unfavorable comments occur in greater variety than favorable. Again this may perhaps mean for any one topic that favorable comments are more group or social and less individual or personal than the unfavorable. One of the most interesting features of this chart is the nature of the comments on supervision in the left-hand diagram. The total number of comments on supervision is 4,662; of these 1,892 were favorable and 2,770 unfavorable. When one remembers how reluctant a worker is to make personal comments on his supervisor, this figure tends to confirm the claim that the interview plan was successful in its attempt to provide avenues for expression of those preoccupations that are better expressed than repressed. Interesting as this chart is, it cannot, however, be regarded as more than a gallant attempt to analyze. According to those who were engaged upon the work, they could cull fragments only from each continuous interview; the continuity itself, the personal and more interesting part, eluded their grasp and escaped. I include the diagram here not merely for its own interest, which is considerable, but also because it gives point to my claim that the interviewing group was beginning to realize that the interview experiment, like the test room, had stumbled upon a group of facts most important for industry, but facts exceedingly difficult to define. Interviewers were uneasily aware that in some indefinable way all was not well with the human situation in the Works.

The situation at first disclosed itself somewhat after this fashion. It was found that comments on material conditions of work had a higher validity than comments on persons. In certain instances a number of persons working in the same vicinity complained of smoke and fumes, or of cold, or of insufficient locker space, or of some other source of irritation. Many of these complaints were found to be just and the specified condition was corrected. But complaints about persons, or for that matter about supervision, in the great majority of instances had to be disregarded. Such complaints served indeed to draw attention to something of interest in the personal history and present attitude of the person being interviewed; but the validity of the external reference was minimal. This led, of course, to some contemporary discussion of the need that industry should develop interviewing technique in order to exploit or anticipate emotional situations. But this was by the way and gave no answer to the leading question.

At the outset, then, the inquiry was baffled, and in two ways. First, one range of facts of which the division, and for that matter management, wished to know more were the facts of inter-personal relation incident to organization and supervision. And these facts when first discovered seemed, alas, to be not facts but prejudiced judgments. The second source of puzzlement was consequent on the first. The interviewing group could not willingly believe that the larger group of persons, of which group they claimed membership, consisted of individuals who were generally unbalanced in their personal judgments. Such a belief was repugnant to common sense and to their social sense. This impasse led to a number of intellectual excursions.

These excursions were undertaken with a view of discovering what avenues had been explored by other inquirers and what solutions such explorers had found of the problem. It was speedily discovered that the special use of the interview which so greatly interested the division was no new thing. Its origin traced to clinical medicine; the Salpêtrière Hospital in Paris had developed it in the study of disordered mentalities; Vienna and Zurich had carried elaboration to the highest power. Bjerre had adapted it to criminal inquiry, Jean Piaget had employed a variant in his studies of children. There is a sentence in the introduction to Piaget's third volume which reads: "The art of the clinician (interviewer) consists not in getting the subject to answer questions but in inducing him to talk freely and to display his spontaneous tendencies in place of cramping them within imposed limits (*i.e.* the limits of a question). It consists in placing every symptom in a mental context, in place of abstracting it from such context." [14] This sentence so closely described the method of interviewing employed at Hawthorne and its object that Piaget's works were eagerly searched for help and direction in the difficult task of relating symptoms to mental contexts. This, however, was but a stage in a long journey.

To summarize: It was clear that there were disabilities of some kind in the Works situation, disabilities that could be mitigated for small groups by the method of the "test room." But this mitigation left the larger question unanswered. The interviewing programme showed that the major difficulty was no mere simple error of supervision, no easily alterable set of working conditions; it

[14] *La Représentation du Monde chez l'Enfant*, Jean Piaget. **Felix Alcan.** Introduction, p. ix.

was something more intimately human, more remote. "Supervision," indeed, had shown itself to be another word which meant so many things that it meant nothing. In every department there was a human situation, these situations were never identical—and in every different situation the supervisor played a different part.

CHAPTER V

THE MEANING OF "MORALE"

BEFORE developing further the course followed by the industrial research, I must at this point briefly sketch the general situation at Hawthorne. The Western Electric Company would stand very high in a list of industrial institutions if the order in such list were determined by consideration of the worker and a real concern for his welfare. In respect of hours of work and wages the Company stands above its compeers. It has provided a restaurant in which good food is obtainable at moderate prices; guests are commonly taken to lunch there by executive authorities and make their selection from food provided for workers. There is an excellently appointed hospital, adequately equipped, and staffed by medical officers of high qualification. The personnel division makes use of every established method of vocational guidance in an effort, which statistics show is highly successful, to suit his work to the worker. There has been no strike or overt symptom of discontent for over twenty years. There can be no question that the general morale, in any accepted meaning of that term, is good and that the Company stands high with its employees. I have not mentioned the various thrift and investment plans which the Company organizes for employees, the vacation provision or numerous other evidences of an unmistakable determination to fulfil humane intention to the utmost.

Any such attempt would require not one chapter but a book, and would not be germane to my topic.

To some extent "the Company," viewed thus, has become almost a mythical entity to workers on the line. There was much evidence of this in the interviews. The first and perhaps the best evidence of the workers' confidence was the unquestioning and immediate acceptance of the Company's assurance of individual anonymity. In the earliest stage each interviewer was asked to repeat to every individual interviewed a few sentences of explanation and assurance as the interview began. Once the programme was established it was often quite difficult for the interviewer to repeat these phrases; the worker wished to brush them aside and begin. In the later phases of the work, when the technique of interviewing had fully developed, it would sometimes chance that a worker, who was full of grievances against supervisors and convinced that he had been unfairly treated, yet did not attribute his ills to the Company. On the contrary he was eager to tell his story, believing that the Company, or some sufficiently remote executive, would offer him redress once his situation was fully known. With respect to the general assurance of anonymity one is happy to be able to add that the interviews have remained inviolate and that the Company has thus justified the confidence of its employees.

It is this situation—a Company definitely committed to justice and humanity in its dealings with workers, the general morale high—that makes the research and its discoveries so interesting. In an industry of low morale and uncertain of its intentions, the inquiry would not have been possible. Only in an industry of the highest standing was it possible to demonstrate the existence of

untouched human problems at depths far below the
superficials of current industrial organization.

Having thus established the perspective of the investigation, I can return to its details. We left the interviewing group embarrassed by the fact that statements
critical of material conditions were fairly reliable, statements critical of persons were not. It was clear that an
easy dichotomy of truth or falsity as applied to statements made in interviews was of small value. The idea
that one might construct from interview material an accurate picture of situations in the Works was frankly
abandoned. The division became convinced that it was
committed to the study of persons and the relations between persons. The interview must be considered as revealing a personality—its history, its attitudes, its merits
and defects. But how to advance beyond the mere
revelation, how to develop from a knowledge-of-ac-
quaintance of persons to a knowledge-about persons and
a method of control—these questions became urgent.

The first clue came from the test rooms. Owing to the
much closer observation of the individual worker that
was part of the pre-arranged routine in the relay assembling and in the mica-splitting experiments, it was possible to relate together personal facts and records of
output in a fashion quite impossible in any general department. Because of this possibility an interesting
observation emerged from study of the first output
records of the mica room. The diagram I show represents
the average hourly output of the individual workers by
successive weeks; I wish to direct attention to the point
where the group has completed the first two experimental
periods and twenty-four weeks of the third period in
which they were given two ten-minute rest-pauses, morn-

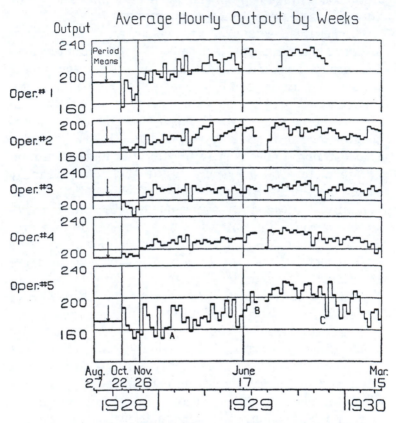

MICA SPLITTING TEST ROOM

(Western Electric Co.-Hawthorne Works-Chicago)

Average Hourly Output by Weeks

Oper.#5: A special instance of the relation between output and personal preoccupation. The points A,B and C relate themselves to changes of personal circumstance, and personal attitude.- (See text)

Oper.#1: A "nervous" case who finally resigns from the Company. Here also there is a pronounced irregularity of output from one week to the next during the period of "overthinking" her personal situation. (See text)

PLATE XI.

ing and afternoon. You will remember that at this time, owing to circumstances which the research division could not control, the group was under heavy pressure, working overtime and frequently on Sunday. In spite of this, the records suggest a certain benefit resulting from the changed industrial milieu and the rest-pauses for the group. Looking a little more closely at the record, however, it is easy to see that the work of numbers one and five shows a pronounced irregularity which at no time characterizes the work of numbers two, three, and four. Consultation of the other records, the history sheets, the log, the original interviews, shows that numbers one and five had been characterized from the first as "nervous." Their ages and experience are widely different: number one was about forty years of age, a widow with two children both doing well at school, she has had five years' experience of splitting mica; number five is eighteen, unmarried, and lives at home, she is "restrained by severe parental discipline, especially from her mother" (a native of Southeastern Europe), she has had a little more than a year's experience of mica splitting. The older woman is intelligent and conscientious, reads and thinks much of "child-welfare," has few friends and is inordinately anxious about her children; in a word, she "overthinks" her situation in true obsessive fashion. The other, the girl, is also heavily preoccupied but in quite a different way. She resents the stern parental control and especially her inability to live as other girls do and to make her own friendships as she will. She does not "overthink" her situation in the active and elaborate fashion of the older woman; in her own less-developed manner she is nevertheless "overthinking" in that she spends her time when not at her most active either resenting the constraint of her elders or suffering "a headache." It is suggestive, though not more than suggestive, that the records of output at a time of heavy pressure for work should show a pronounced irregularity in the records of two out of five operatives, those two who are known, by comparison with the other three, to be heavily preoccupied with a personal situation.

Both of these workers suffer from insufficient social contact, an inadequate social inter-relation with other people. In the case of the older woman, personal factors were doubtless involved which precluded the possibility of any simple adjustive remedy. In the case of the younger the difficulty centred in an external interference, a constraint which, however admirable in Southeastern Europe, was anomalous in a suburb of Chicago and operated merely to close down every avenue of happy activity and personal development. In the latter case, therefore, there was a possibility of benefit from the improved social atmosphere of the experimental room with its freedom from constraint and pleasant chatter as there was not in the case of the older woman. Second, I want to call attention to the effect upon the younger worker of rather more than a year of association with new-found comrades in the test room. Her record can be roughly divided into three periods: first, a period (Plate XI, point A) in which the irregularity is at its highest with little or no improvement—about twenty-three weeks; second, a period of reduced irregularity and slight improvement (Plate XI, A to B)—about nineteen weeks; and third, a period of no significant irregularity and much higher production—about fifteen weeks to the end of 1929 (Plate XI, point C). In the first of these periods, her talk—spontaneous—to her colleagues takes the form of personal complaint, a headache, or perhaps her personal situation. In the second period the whole group is aware of the problem between herself and her mother, but takes it calmly and as what the anthropologists call a "clash of cultures" rather than a personal situation. This not merely gives her a sense of comradeship and social support; it also operates to diminish the factor of personal resentment and exaggeration in the situation. Towards the end of this period she discovers—obviously to her astonishment—that the remedy is in her own hands; she has enough money to live on and comfortably, she can transfer herself to living quarters with some girl friend. The determination to do this and the actual transfer are the unseen accompaniments of the sustained improvement of the third period.

Now if the research division and the officers of the Company had not arranged for the observation of other changes than those in the area of immediate experiment, it is obvious that the changes here presented in an output curve would probably have been credited directly to the changed working conditions in the test room or to a "learning curve." Indirectly, of course, her improvement is due to the change, but so very indirectly that it cannot be entirely credited to rest-pauses or even to the improvement in human atmosphere. The change is an outcome of social comradeship and discussion in some degree; more than this, it is due to a consequential and major change in method of living. The changed method of living not only frees the worker from a perpetual interference with her personal development—unjustified by anything in the Chicago adolescent milieu; it also puts her in a position such that she can talk to her immediate relatives and seniors on a footing of greater comparative equality. That the separation was chiefly effective finds demonstration in subsequent events. After some time, the economic situation compelled this girl to return to living with her family. Subsequent to this her output curve once again descended and developed something of its former irregularity. This, in spite of the fact that for some time after this the conditions in the experimental room were maintained. Further discussion of this interesting case and similar cases will be found in the official reports which are now being prepared for publication by F. J. Roethlisberger, of the Industrial Research Department at Harvard, with H. A. Wright and W. J. Dickson, research officers of the Western Electric Company.

This was not the only instance discovered by the research division of the relation between output, morale, and heavy personal preoccupation. It is, however, the instance which best lends itself to comparatively objective demonstration before an audience. It had become clear to the interviewing department that, in those many instances where personal situations of this or some similar type were divulged in the intimate anonymity of an interview, it was fair to assume the existence of a condition of affairs essentially similar to that which had revealed itself in the mica room. It was evident that such persons would be less well able to support pressure of any kind than those more fortunately placed. "Pressure" in this use must be interpreted to mean much more than, for example, merely working overtime; indifferent supervisory methods, unfriendliness in fellow workers, monotonous or repetitive work, all these would possibly serve to provoke a distorted interpretation, an irrational response. In something of this fashion did the interviewing group begin its effort to understand the questionable reliability of personal comments in the interviews. A comment in one interview reads "Between the hard luck at home and the unfair treatment round here (*i.e.* in the Works), why I certainly feel 'dumpy' many a day." With respect to comments of this type, and they were not infrequent, the division began to believe:

1. Such an individual—hard luck at home and feeling "dumpy"—is not a reliable judge of departmental conditions.

2. He is probably caught in a vicious circle; he feels "dumpy" in any event and consequently every event is interpreted to increase his conviction of hard luck and unfair treatment.

3. One cannot "handle" such an individual adequately without understanding his history, his present circumstance, and so his method of thinking and consequent attitude.

Janet's investigation of obsessive thinking was the first study which contributed to redirection of the inquiry.

There is one variety of psychoneurotic ill which by the evidence of all the schools of psychopathology seems to be unmistakably a mental ill—a trouble that originates in circumstance and defective education in the broadest sense. This is the affliction described as obsession by the French school and as compulsion neurosis by the Freudians. It alone seems free from suspicion of organic pathological complication as hysteria and the psychoses are not. It alone is clearly curable, in numerous instances, by reëducation or psychological "analysis." The chief character of this complaint is described by both the above-quoted terms, the individual is unable to control his reflective thinking—he is "obsessed" by certain ideas which seem to him to have a "compulsive" power of establishing themselves in his preoccupations even though he believes such ideas to be irrational or untrue. In extreme cases the mental ill is serious; in a milder form the trouble penetrates the whole fabric of our civilization and probably constitutes the chief mental disability of our time. Two English investigators, to whose work I have previously referred, Dr. Millais Culpin and Dr. May Smith, have published an inquiry into the incidence of this type of ill in industry under the title of "The Nervous Temperament." [1] They describe the special characteristics of the mildly obsessive individual as follows: "Symptoms chiefly characterized in consciousness by unreasonable drive. The sufferer says he is forced to think certain thoughts. . . . The penalty for fighting against them, even when that is possible, is great stress. . . . The language used by people having such symptoms nearly always contains suggestions of the literal meaning (*i.e.* of obsession); it is of the nature of a hostile siege; something against their own will takes possession temporarily and forces their thoughts in a particular direction. . . . It is not easy to detect these people, for their symptoms may not be expressed in unusual behavior. . . . They rarely display their mental state; they believe strongly in the power and importance of self-control, which they exercise consciously in various directions. They tend to overwork, and give the impression of taking the line of greatest resistance. When a breakdown comes it is usually ascribed to overwork though the overwork itself is a symptom and not the cause of the state. . . . Obsessional subjects tend to be intellectually superior, some occupy-

[1] I. F. R. B., Report No. 61, 1930.

ing important positions; yet their mental conflicts, in which they use up much energy, seem to prevent them from attaining their highest possible efficiency." [2]

Later, describing the typical behavior of an obsessive who occupies an important position, Culpin and Smith say: "He knows the liability to error and so checks his work, but while he may have an intellectual conviction that it is quite right, he has no emotional satisfaction. He will be forced to go over it again and again. . . . If he is master of his own time and there is nothing to prevent him from checking as often as he is impelled, he carries on well and gains among his colleagues an almost religious veneration for hard work; but if he should be in a business firm where he has to give up his work at the demand of others, his mental stress is very great and breakdown will be almost unavoidable. . . . Obsessive *acts* are described in textbooks as marking severe cases, but in this investigation obsessive *thoughts* have been more frequently elicited. Their nature and significance are difficult to grasp without actual experience of more severe cases; they are liable to be missed, but when disclosed are quite definite. . . . The close relation between their presence (*i.e.* obsessive thoughts) and an excellent dotting record (*i.e.* in a test) is remarkable. . . ." [3]

The respective attitudes of the French and German schools of psychopathology to this pathology of thinking are quite different. Contrary to the common supposition, there is no inherent irreconcilability in the two descriptions; they are rather complementary. The French school, especially its founder and chief exponent, Pierre Janet, is chiefly interested in the manner of obsessive thinking; the German school is interested in what the

[2] *Op. cit.*, p. 10.   [3] *Ibid.*, p. 11.

obsessive is thinking about and how he came to think it. Janet better than any other psychopathologist is able to describe minutely the technical defects in the obsessive's control of his thought processes at the moment of his acutest difficulty; Freud is content to trace the development of his insufficient or perverse ideas and compulsive rituals back to the circumstances and morbid preoccupation of an unhappy infancy.

Janet's two important treatises, from the standpoint of a student of industry and society, are *Les Obsessions et la Psychasthénie*[4] and *Les Névroses*.[5] The latter is a small book in which he summarizes his findings on both hysteria and obsession. In these studies he insists, and illustrates freely from case material, that the chief characteristic of obsession is an utter incapacity to respond adequately to any present situation and especially to a social situation. Even when alone these subjects are afraid of, and avoid, anything of the nature of decision or action. In describing this incapacity in greater detail, Janet first points to the highly organized and complex equilibrium involved in any ordinary act of attention in the normal person. It is customary to speak of attention as if it were essentially a simple fact—the characteristic unit, as it were, of mental life. We make this assumption because the individual of normal organic and mental health easily concentrates upon this or that aspect of the world about him without ever realizing how complex are the controls he takes for granted. Our mental life, says Janet, "not only consists of a succession of phenomena coming one after the other and forming a long series . . . but each of these successive states is in reality a complex state; it contains a multitude of elementary facts and

[4] Paris, Felix Alcan, 1919.   [5] Flammarion, Paris, 1930.

owes its apparent unity to synthesis alone, to the equilibrium of all these elements." [6] Since it is only by means of attention, and the organization it presumes, that we can actively relate ourselves to the reality about us, it follows that any individual in whom this capacity is in any degree diminished, but whose mentality is otherwise undamaged, experiences a feeling of incompleteness and unreality which makes him still more miserably aware of his difference from, and inferiority to, other people. Janet points out that obsessives are "perpetually distracted"; they have great difficulty in attending or "putting order into their ideas." [7] Difficulty of "fixing and sustaining attention" is "their chief trouble." There may be an exaggeration of spontaneous attention with a weakening of voluntary attention—when they begin to do some simple act they find it difficult to stop. [8] The constant re-checking of their work mentioned by Culpin and Smith is thus always present as a symptom. Such subjects are very doubtful of descriptive studies in which there is some question of fact; they prefer ideas and above all abstract ideas. [9] They are very fond of lengthy discussions that range back and forth and get nowhere. They dislike physiology but are addicts of psychology; [10] they become terrible metaphysicians. [11] Their inability to order their various capacities in such a fashion that attention is facilitated leaves them with a diminished "function of the real," in Janet's phrase; apart from this their malady "leaves intact intellectual operations properly so-called." [12] From this derives their awareness of their incapacity and, at any moment of inability to act,

---

[6] *L'État Mental des Hystériques*, Pierre Janet, Paris, Alcan, p. 425.
[7] *Les Obs.*, p. 371. [10] *Les Obs.*, p. 360.
[8] *Les Obs.*, p. 353. [11] *Les Névroses*, p. 357.
[9] *Les Obs.*, p. 360. [12] *Les Obs.*, p. 749.

the consequent crises of revery.[18] The term "agonies of indecision" was unquestionably coined by someone intimately acquainted with the obsessive habit of mind. An obsessive soldier when asked if he would like to remove to another hospital remained rigid and unsleeping for eight hours because he could not decide; finally he asked the military doctor to decide for him. Another, a woman, asked casually in hospital by a visitor if she "felt better," pondered a possible reply for three hours after her visitor had gone and then suffered an emotional collapse. This same patient, while out for a walk, turned into a small park, then spent the remainder of the morning walking round and round, finally weeping as she walked, because she could not decide to go out. They are "scrupulous" to the minutest point; the burden of decision is the burden of possible sin. They are experts in an arduous re-thinking of the obvious—they substitute an exaggerated precision in minor activities for that activity in major affairs of which they are, or feel themselves to be, incapable.

This type of study had, of course, no direct interest for the interviewing group. It might have been expected that any so intimate approach to the individual as the interview had become would have resulted, even in the comparatively short space of a two-hour talk, in the discovery of numerous obsessives. I think it is fair to say that amongst the whole twenty thousand persons interviewed, not more than perhaps a round dozen revealed themselves as unmistakable candidates for the psychiatrist. But the inquiry was at no time directed to the discovery of the mentally afflicted; it was rather interested in a question as to the source of a tendency to ex-

[18] *Les Név.,* p. 79.

aggeration and distortion in statements made by sufficiently normal people. The interest of the research group in Janet derived from the fact that he is at some pains, first, to show that in veritable cases of obsession the patient occasionally takes charge of a situation in emergency and is without symptoms for the period. One of Janet's most remarkable patients was free from all indecision, crises of revery, or other disability during three months of a domestic crisis, relapsing later when the urgent need for action had passed.[14] Second, Janet demonstrates at length that a person who is not in any sense an obsessive will nevertheless respond obsessively to any experience of obvious personal inadequacy in a situation which is to him important. Any sufficiently wholesale disturbance of an individual's personal equilibrium with the reality about him will tend to carry an obsessive consequence in his thinking. The provoking occasion may be an organic unbalance, one of the fatigues; or it may be a social experience of personal futility. In either event he will display for the time being the obsessive revery, the elaborate indecision, the morbid preoccupation with unreal personal issues. If he cannot adequately "think through" the situation to amended action, he will proceed to "overthink" his situation in terms of false alternatives, just as the obsessive does.[15] For the period of such disturbance, even the most capable individual will lose his usual control both of attentive capacity and of reflection or revery. He will suffer a diminished power of quick adaptation to actual situations, especially the social; he will be unable, for the time being, to prevent himself from thinking in an exaggerated and distorted fashion about himself and other people.

[14] *Les Obs.,* p. 548.   [15] *Les Név.,* pp. 360, 361.

Janet's demonstration of the mentally shattering effect of an experience of personal incapacity seemed to provide a possible clue to a better interpretation of the distorted statements about persons in many interviews. The research division, subsequent to its perusal of Janet, was led to propound two questions:

> (1) Is some experience which might be described as an experience of personal futility a common incident of industrial organization for work?

> (2) Does life in a modern industrial city in some unrealized way predispose workers to obsessive response?

These two questions in some form continued to preoccupy those in charge of the research until the conclusion of the inquiry.

The former of these questions at first engaged the attention of the division. It found some support in the numerous tales of supervisory misinterpretation and misunderstanding told in the interviews. Sometimes these stories had preoccupied a worker's mind for years without finding any opportunity of adequate expression. The experience of the two experimental rooms tended also to confirm the hypothesis that conditions of work tended in some way to prevent rather than facilitate a satisfactory personal adaptation. The many comments made by the girl operatives of both test rooms, over a period of years, all seemed to express relief from some previously experienced constraint or "interference." Particular instances of a personal unbalance of some type finding expression as criticism of Company policy also came to light. Early in the history of the test-room study, one of the operatives suddenly became restless and openly expressed her dislike of the experiment. She was permitted to withdraw and a substitute was found. Later, in reconsidering this incident, it was noticed that a physical examination of the original worker had shown her red-blood cell count to be low and her hæmoglobin percentage only sixty-eight. The officer in charge sought her out, explained that she was anæmic and offered her medical assistance. Reëxamination showed a slightly lower cell count and much the same hæmoglobin percentage. Under medical treatment she rapidly recovered in respect of both cell count and hæmoglobin percentage and in subsequent discussion disavowed her former criticisms of the Company. She added that at the time of making these criticisms she was suffering a "feeling of fatigue"—which was considered possibly to have been indicative of her organic disability.

Simultaneously with the development of interest in the first question stated above, some tentative moves had been made in the direction suggested by the second; that, namely, as to the effect of life in a modern industrial centre upon individual capacity and attitude. Janet, for all his descriptive excellence with respect to any present situation, nowhere concerns himself with the origin in different individuals of the tendency to irrational thinking or mild melancholy. The research division had accordingly given some attention to Freudian theories of the importance of personal history; it had also given even more attention to recent developments in social anthropology. A representative of the Harvard Department of Anthropology had called attention to the logical insufficiency of a merely psychological study of the individuals in a department. Laboratory and clinical psychological studies are interested in the individual—his vocational capacity or incapacity, his social "adjustment" or "maladjustment." These studies are, and always will be, exceedingly important; but they do no more than touch the fringe of human inquiry. The individuals who make up a working department are not merely individuals; they constitute a group within which individuals have developed routines of relationship to each other, to their superiors, to their work, and to the policies of the Company. A high incidence of so-called "social maladjustment" in a given group may refer itself to something in these routine relationships to the work and to each other rather than to some primary irrationality in the individual. Interviewers had noticed that an individual who is not very capable, or not very well adjusted socially, may behave capably and normally when he works in a human surrounding that suits and sustains him. And, on the contrary, an exceedingly capable and normal human being will behave as if he were neither when he works in inappropriate surroundings. The two experimental rooms confirmed this hypothesis—that the locus of industrial maladjustment is somewhere in the relation between person—work—Company policy rather than in any individual or individuals. In two instances, newly organized departments showed a high incidence of the personal futility type of statement in interviews, and in both instances it was clear that no sufficiently simply patterned group relationship to work had been developed.

Simultaneously with this development in its thinking, the research division, by now accepted as representing a new method of inquiry into situations, was asked to undertake a study of a particular department. Certain of the most experienced interviewers, equipped with a technique derived from several years of work and critical reflection, were detailed to the task. The situation that disclosed itself when studied in this way was so interesting that the attention of the research group was brought back from personality and personal history to the industrial situation itself. Thus commenced the final phase of the Western Electric inquiry, the phase in which it began to be possible to plot tentatively the relation of the findings of interviewers to the discoveries of the test rooms, and the significance of both for Company policy.

It is important that I should be clear as to the actual difference in procedures involved in the new plan. In the original programme interviewers were set to conduct interviews throughout the various departments which together constituted the Inspection Branch of sixteen hundred people; in the first development beyond this, a larger body of interviewers, making use of a developed technique, worked over the various departments which together constituted the Operating Branch of ten thousand people. Under the general arrangements made in this phase, the interviews that came into the headquarters of the division on any given day for record and consideration bore no definable or easily traceable relation to each other or to the actual industrial situation. *This method was inevitably weighted in the direction of an emphasis upon personal irrationality because any personal criticism or complaint was voiced merely by a letter and number in the files and could not possibly be balanced against any countervailing study of the actualities of the human situation in the department criticized.* The innovation in method which I am now describing was to set one or two interviewers to continuous study of the individuals in a department day by day and week by week, and to ask the investigators to develop simultaneously by direct observation the appropriate knowledge of the inter-relationships and activities of the group as a whole. This had the effect of demonstrating not only the meaning *in a specified situation* of an expressed dislike or criticism, but also the reasoned adequacy or otherwise of such expression.

The interviewers and observers detailed to this task found no difficulty in the undertaking. The research division and its methods of inquiry had been generally accepted; no obstacles were put in its way. One interviewer thus engaged comments in his first report (Nov. 9, 1931, to March 18, 1932) upon the need to establish a sufficiently intimate personal relationship between the investigators and the working group. He continues: "We have been able to develop this relationship quite rapidly, largely because of an open-minded attitude on the part of the supervisors. They seem to be quite willing to talk their problems over with us. The employees also have been unbelievably frank . . . the observer is being included in conversations which are materially altered with the approach of the supervisors." In this situation it was not difficult for the investigators to make observations which seemed to provide a more adequate definition of the significant problems. The condition of affairs which revealed itself was not at all that which might have been expected. There was no great evidence of that "deadening" effect of machine minding or routine work which literary critics commonly suppose to be the chief problem of a mechanical age. There was no reason to suppose that the personal or human quality of the supervision was essentially defective. But many "conflicting forces and attitudes" were "working at cross-purposes with each other." This conflict centred about "the focal point" of an industrial situation; namely, the work and the manner of its performance. Somehow or other, no effective relationship between "the worker and his work" had been established; and since a community of interest at this point was lacking the group failed to establish an integrate activity and fell into a degree of discord which no one could understand or control.

In a particular instance it was found that neither the supervisors nor any of the working group really knew the "bogey" that had been set nor the facts considered in its determination. They did not clearly understand the method of payment on the job. The whole department echoed with protective devices, some of which were known to the supervisor and others not so known. On a first observation there was a tendency to ascribe this to an alleged habit of "restricting output"; it was speedily found that this phrase expresses a gross simplification which is essentially untrue. Apparently it is not enough to have an enlightened Company policy, a carefully devised (and blue-printed) plan of manufacture. To stop at this point, and merely administer such plan, however logical, to workers with a take-it-or-leave-it attitude has much the same effect as administering medicine to a recalcitrant patient. It may be good for him, but he is not persuaded. If an individual cannot work with sufficient understanding of his work situation, then, unlike a machine, he can only work against opposition from himself. This is the essential nature of the human; with all the will in the world to coöperate, he finds it difficult to persist in action for an end he cannot dimly see. From this it follows that the more intelligent an industrial method, the more difficulty does it encounter in performance and action. This is because if intelligent it changes as a method in response to externally dictated need or with the progress of invention—and fails to carry its workers intelligently with it. Many varieties of situation were discovered at Hawthorne, but wherever the symptoms described as "restriction" clearly showed themselves, something of exasperation or a sense of personal futility was also revealed. There was a conflict of loyalties—to the Company, to the supervisor, to the working group—and no possibility of solution, except by improved understanding. Whether they admitted "stalling" or no, workers expressed their dislike for a situation which imposed upon them a constraint and a disloyalty. Evidently the more intelligent a company policy, the more necessary is it that there shall be a method of communicating understanding "down the line." And this method of communication must include the interview— that is, it must know and effectively meet the real difficulties which workers themselves experience and express, and must take account also of personal disability.

At this point in the inquiry a relation had established itself between the "interview programme" and the results obtained in the experimental rooms. The source of those constraints, relief from which the relay assemblers had so freely expressed, had, at least in part, revealed itself. Human collaboration in work, in primitive and developed societies, has always depended for its perpetuation upon the evolution of a non-logical social code which regulates the relations between persons and their attitudes to one another. Insistence upon a merely economic logic of production—especially if the logic is frequently changed— interferes with the development of such a code and consequently gives rise in the group to a sense of human defeat. This human defeat results in the formation of a social code at a lower level and in opposition to the economic logic. One of its symptoms is "restriction." In its devious road to this enlightenment, the research division had learned something of the personal exasperation caused by a continual experience of incomprehension and futility. It had also learned how serious a consequence such experience carries for industry and for the individual.

CHAPTER VI

THE REACTION OF INDUSTRY UPON THE SOCIAL ORDER. TECHNICAL DEVELOPMENT AND *ANOMIE*

In the last three chapters I have briefly described the Hawthorne researches of the Western Electric Company—the course that the investigation ran, its tentative findings. I hope that other large companies will set themselves as intelligently, and with as unmistakable a social purpose, to discover something of the human situations that exist in factory and workshop. At this point, however, our adventure moves outside the Works and into the rapidly changing modern industrial community. There is a question formulated by the research division at Hawthorne which we take with us, the second of the two stated in the last chapter: Does life in a modern industrial centre in some unrealized way predispose workers to obsessive response? We may take it as decided that it is far too easily possible for an intelligent worker to experience something of futility and exasperation in modern industry and business, although little can as yet be said of its occasion.

Outside the Works at Hawthorne, we move into Cicero and Chicago, into areas which have been closely studied by Professor Robert E. Park and his colleagues of the University of Chicago. These studies taken as a group constitute one of the most interesting contributions to the social knowledge of our time; they have not yet been

122

recognized for what they are and used as they should
be. One method of study employed is in effect anthropological; it takes account geographically of a residential
area and investigates the cultural influence of such area
upon its inhabitants, and its functional relation as an
area to the greater Chicago. Of all these studies none
possesses more immediate interest than Clifford Shaw's
"Delinquency Areas." [1] This is a "study of the geo-
graphic distribution (place of residence) of delinquents
in Chicago" during the years between 1917 and 1927. It
is "based upon separate studies of eight series of individual offenders, including 5,159 male school truants,
43,298 juvenile delinquents, and 7,541 adult offenders, a
total of 55,998 individuals." [2] The home addresses of the
individual offenders in each of the eight series were
spotted on a map of Chicago. These maps were divided
into zones, square-mile areas, and in various other ways
subjected to study.

Chicago is perhaps unlike older cities in that its geographical arrangement still reflects its rapid growth. It
possesses a business centre and shopping district, commonly known as the Loop, outside this an industrial area
and a confusion of slum dwellings, beyond this again is
a workers' residential area, and still farther out a residential area of a more prosperous type. Moving along a
"radial" from the centre, the Loop, one therefore moves
through a stratification in a cultural sense, passing from
business and professional activity to industry and slum,
and then through residences which grow better with each
remove. This is not absolute, of course, but perhaps more
characteristic of Chicago than of cities elsewhere. At the
time when the study was in progress, Chicago was prob-

[1] Univ. of Chicago Press, 1929.   [2] *Loc. cit.*, p. 22.

ably the most suitable city that could have been selected. By reason of its enormous growth and the extreme rapidity of such growth it manifested clearly some of the immediate effects of industrial development upon the social order. The selection was therefore most appropriate, even if it be true that in Chicago such effects are also exaggerated.

After the home addresses of the individual offenders had been spotted on the Chicago map, "the next step in the study was to compute the rate or the ratio of offenders to the total population of similar age and sex in the different areas of the city, so that comparisons between areas could be made. This ratio, expressed in terms of the number of offenders per hundred individuals of the same age and sex," [3] was designated throughout the study as "the rate of individual delinquents." Shaw's various series do not all cover the same years but occur within the specified period. In addition to four series covering boys of ten to sixteen years of age, he has one of males between seventeen and twenty (6,398), another of "adult offenders" between seventeen and seventy-five (7,541) and still another series which studies a group of girl delinquents between the ages of ten and seventeen (2,869). His typical finding in all these series I illustrate by quoting his delinquent rate for Series VI. This series is an examination of the geographical distribution (residence) of 6,398 male offenders between the ages of seventeen and twenty brought before the Boys' Court in Chicago on felony charges in the years 1924, 1925, and 1926. A special map of Chicago is prepared by describing concentric circles, or arcs of circles, separated from each other by a distance representing a mile—the Loop being

[3] *Loc. cit.*, p. 25.

taken as centre. The rates for each successive zone thus described and moving outwards from the business and industrial centre are: for Zone I nearest the Loop, 25.1, Zone II 16.3, Zone III 15.5, Zone IV 10.1, Zone V 7.5, Zone VI 5.3, Zone VII 4.7, Zone VIII 3.8, Zone IX 3.8. This is his characteristic finding; a high rate, 25 per cent of individuals of the same sex and age, near the industrial centre, a comparatively low rate, 3.8 per cent, on the residential periphery of Chicago.[4] He states his findings thus:

"1. The first and perhaps most striking finding of the study is that there are marked variations in the rate of school truants, juvenile delinquents, and adult criminals between areas in Chicago. Some areas are characterized by very high rates, while others show very low rates."[5]

"2. A second major finding is that rates of truancy, delinquency, and adult crime tend to vary inversely in proportion to the distance from the centre of the city (p. 202). In Chicago the nearer a residential locality is to the centre of the city, the higher its rate of delinquency and crime."

"3. Another striking finding in this study is the marked similarity in the distribution of truants, juvenile delinquents, and adult criminals in the city. Those communities which show the highest rates of juvenile delinquency also show, as a rule, the highest rates of truancy and adult crime."

"4. A fourth finding of this study is that the difference in rates of truancy, delinquency, and crime reflect differences in community backgrounds. . . . In this study we have not attempted to correlate delinquency rates with specific social factors, but we have indicated in a

[4] *Loc. cit.,* p. 115.　　　　　[5] *Loc. cit.,* p. 198.

general way that there are characteristic social conditions which accompany crime and delinquency."

"5. In this connection it is interesting to note that the main high rate areas of the city—those near the Loop, around the Stock Yards, and the South Chicago steel mills—have been characterized by high rates over a long period. . . . It should be remembered that relatively high rates have persisted in certain areas notwithstanding the fact that the composition of population has changed markedly." [6]

In attempting a tentative interpretation of these observations, Shaw says: "It has been quite common in discussions of delinquency to attribute causal significance to such conditions as poor housing, overcrowding, low living standards, low educational standards, and so on. But these conditions themselves probably reflect a type of community life. By treating them one treats only symptoms of more basic processes. . . . In short, with the process of growth of the city, the invasion of residential communities by business and industry causes a disintegration of the community as a unit of social control. This disorganization is intensified by the influx of foreign national and racial groups whose old cultural and social controls break down in the new cultural and racial situation of the city. . . ." [7]

According to Clifford Shaw, delinquency and criminality are symptoms of the disintegration of social controls. Since misunderstanding is possible, it is necessary to point out that Shaw does not mean the kind of control exercised by another person, by a court of law, or a legislative mandate. He means the inner compulsion to think and act in a way that is socially acceptable, a compulsion

[6] *Loc. cit.*, p. 203.   [7] *Loc. cit.*, p. 205.

which is imposed upon an ordered community by social tradition. This is the only compulsion that is ever really operative in a social group; courts and their principal officers or legislative enactments are effective only when they express an implication of an accepted and traditional method of living.

Shaw calls attention to the fact that an increase of delinquency and crime is indicative of disintegration in those social controls which are necessary to ordered living and progress. But these are not the only symptoms. Dr. Cavan in her study of the incidence of suicide in Chicago [8] is also able to use maps similar to those used by Shaw and to demonstrate that the rate of suicide is highest in those areas which show other evidence of social disorganization. There is not a complete coincidence with the Shaw areas, because in Chicago, as in other communities, occupational groups of a professional type, for example, show a comparatively high suicide rate. This lack of complete coincidence is, however, of special interest because the Cavan hypothesis, that "personal disorganization" follows a breakdown in community organization, finds confirmation even with respect to the professional instances in special case studies. Delinquency and crime are evidence mainly of gross breakdown; it does not follow that a relative freedom from gross breakdown indicates immunity to social disintegration.

Cavan states her conclusions as follows: . . . "in communities organized on a religious basis and in small towns and rural sections the suicide rate is low, apparently both because the old traditional attitudes against suicide are still held there, and because there is little occasion for confusion of interests and purposes. Cities,

[8] "Suicide," Ruth Shonle Cavan, Univ. of Chicago Press, 1928.

on the other hand, tend to be in a perpetual state of disorganization, and the multiplicity of contacts and diverse codes of conduct permit liberation of the individual from traditional ways of thinking and at the same time often make it almost impossible for him to achieve satisfactory relationships for the fulfilment of his interests."

"The relationship of suicide to social disorganization is further evident in the contrast between preliterate and civilized groups. . . . A similar contrast is seen in the conditions of European peoples and of European immigrants in American cities, whose rates of suicide are two or three times as high as in their parent-countries."

"Perhaps in the study of suicide in Chicago the relation between personal and social disorganization is best illustrated. The two terms are not synonymous but they denote related phenomena. Social disorganization is the loss of control of the mores over the members of the group. A certain amount of social disorganization does not disrupt the group, and is in fact common to all but the most static groups. Persons who are uncontrolled by the mores may be personally disorganized, or they may have elaborated a more or less individual scheme of behavior which permits satisfaction of interests, and an efficient life. . . . It is true, however, that when social disorganization exists there is liable to be a greater amount of personal disorganization than in a stable community. . . . When the social organization disintegrates . . . people are often unable to formulate for themselves substitute attitudes and habits." [9]

There are many of us who tend to think of the alleged "new freedom" in act and thought, possessed by an individual in a modern society, as clear gain. Such thinking

[9] *Loc. cit.*, pp. 330, 331.

is heedless of two facts: these are, first, that a diminished social control demands an accession of intelligent self-control and, second, that any movement in the direction of this so-called freedom withdraws from the individual a measure of social understanding and support which he is usually unable to do without. Cavan and Shaw show us some of the symptoms—delinquency, crime, and suicide—of social disorganization: we have to understand that the ill in some degree afflicts the whole social body and not merely the specified areas of Chicago. We are looking at one aspect of a change which is affecting the life of modern communities, strongly in the United States, but as certainly, if less strongly, in Europe.

Nearly forty years have elapsed since Durkheim, an eminent sociologist of France, published his famous study of suicide. His book has usually been accepted at its face value and critically considered as a sociological and statistical attempt to present the facts with respect to suicide for different localities and different countries. At the hands of modern sociologists and statisticians it has not fared very well. Careful reading, however, shows that the use made by Durkheim of his facts and figures was incidental only to his main purpose. His main purpose even in the year 1897 was to show that an industrial civilization, in proportion as it undergoes rapid development, tends to suffer from an ill which he terms *anomie*— anomia. This has sometimes been literally translated as "lawlessness"—which does not quite express Durkheim's meaning. His central claim is, first, that a small society lives in an ordered manner such that the interests of its members are subordinated to the interest of the group. He does not mean anything that is political or, in any explicit sense, moral by this subordination. His reference is rather to the fact that an individual born as member of such a community can, during infancy and adolescence, see ahead of him the function he will unquestionably fulfil for the group when he is adult. This anticipation regulates his thought and action in the developing years, and in adulthood culminates in satisfaction and a sense of function for, and necessity to, the society. He is throughout his life *solidaire* with the group.[10] Modern development, Durkheim claims, has brought to an end this life of satisfactory function for the individual and the group. We are facing a condition of *anomie*, of planlessness in living, which is becoming characteristic both of individual lives and of communities. This is due, at least in part, to economic development. "For so long as a producer could only dispose of his products in the immediate vicinity, the moderate gain possible did not greatly overexcite his ambition. But now that he can almost claim to have the whole world for customer how, before so unlimited a prospect, can his ambition continue to accept its former limitation?"[11] Durkheim contends that individuals increasingly are lapsing into restless movement, planless self-development—a method of living which defeats itself because achievement has no longer any criterion of value; happiness always lies beyond any present achievement. Defeat takes the form of ultimate disillusion—a disgust with the "futility of endless pursuit."

I quote from Durkheim in order to show that the problems which concern Shaw and Cavan are not peculiar to Chicago. It is true that the problem of social disorganization, with its consequent *anomie*, probably exists in a more acute form in Chicago than in other parts of

[10] *Le Suicide*, Paris, Felix Alcan, 1897, p. 277.   [11] *Op. cit.*, p. 284.

the United States. It is probable that it is a more immediate issue in the United States than in Europe. But it is a problem of order in social development with which the whole world is concerned.

Another contribution to the study, in this instance more directly pointed at the individual, comes from Freud and that development of psychopathology for which he is in large part responsible. We are not concerned here with those detailed aspects of his theory which have roused controversy in the psychopathic clinics of the world. We are rather interested in the general implications of his special approach and method. In his first approach to the problem of obsession or compulsive thinking, Freud adopted the view that the patient suffered "mostly from reminiscences," especially reminiscences of some former unfortunate experience in which his emotions had been unable to find adequate social expression.[12] This so-called "abreaction" theory stated the need that such patients should fully recall and express the pathological incident and its emotion; it is unquestionably true of some cases. Mental specialists found this idea of great service in dealing with the so-called "shell-shock" symptoms of those who suffered horrifying and unusual experiences in the World War. Those interviews at Hawthorne in which an individual expressed great relief after he had circumstantially described a misunderstanding of years before, seem also to relate themselves to this theory. The "abreaction" theory, however, was only a first attempt with but a limited application, and Freud passed quickly to that conception of nervous ills which is now associated with his name.[13] He points

[12] Selected Papers, Nervous and Mental Monographs, No. 4, pp. 5 *ff*.
[13] Three Contributions, Nervous and Mental Monographs, No. 7, third edition, pp. 4 *ff*.

out that in the majority of instances abnormality of mental attitude reflects "disturbances" which have occurred during the infantile "developmental period." [14] No longer does he interpret these disturbances as symptomatic merely of insufficiently expressed emotion or of "defence" against such reminiscences. He claims rather that the disturbed or abnormal surrounding in infancy has been responsible for a distortion of desire and that the neurosis is the negative expression of the distorted tendency; that is to say, it is due to an attempt to suppress a distortion. His central thesis is that the appropriate repression of perverse tendencies must be established in the infantile period, since any attempt to establish such limitations after puberty will inevitably find neurotic expression.

Putting aside the stern Old Testament morality involved in this—Jeremiah's complaint that "the heart is deceitful above all things and desperately wicked"—if this be put aside, the doctrine becomes very much what the mental hygiene movement in the United States has made it. In all the early stages of his development the child requires a normally constituted home and family affection; he needs also and equally the companionship of other children of his own age under the conditions afforded by an ordered society. The unit of social explanation is not the human individual, nor is it the family; it is a group of families living in an ordered relation with each other. Freud has succeeded in showing that the obsessive is socially maladjusted, that his attitude even to his own family is peculiar and distorted. Further investigation shows that the family which produces him is itself inadequately related to the communal life.

[14] *Loc. cit.,* pp. 9 *ff.*

The effect of Freud's inquiry is therefore to demonstrate that the maladjustment of the neurotic is a social maladjustment; his disability is not an individual but a social problem. The symptoms of sex obsession which his clinical method pursues with such tenacity are the consequence, and only the consequence, of a primary social disruption. If we disregard the controversial aspects of his theory we are most certainly entitled to conclude from his inquiries that any social situation which shows extensive disorganization will also show a higher tendency to obsession in its individual members than an ordered community. This will not necessarily find expression merely in a greater number of extreme cases; it will also show itself in the form of a higher incidence of obsessive thinking in those who otherwise are sufficiently "well-adjusted" and sufficiently capable of social living. It is the fashion to treat the former of these—the increasing number of "cases"—as a major problem of our time; the latter may conceivably be the more urgent.

The psychopathic inquiry is, however, a somewhat negative method of obtaining the requisite evidence. Psychiatry is one of the most important studies of today; it will nevertheless fail of effect unless it be supplemented by direct social investigation. Durkheim's modern representative and critic, Professor Maurice Halbwachs, thus expresses his view: "Social life offers us the spectacle of an effort eternally renewed by human groups to triumph over the causes of disintegration which threaten such groups. The weapons of society in this struggle are collective beliefs and customs. When these are weakened or shaken, it can be claimed that the vital resources of the group are reduced. For the rest the causes of disintegration are disabilities of function such as may occur in any complex machine, in any delicate organism; they are due to the structure of the organism or of the machine. Should these disabilities multiply or the effort of the society weaken—and both may occur simultaneously, especially during the passage from an ancient and traditional type of life to a new and more complex civilization—then we shall see breaks appear in the social structure. It is somewhere within such breaks that one looks for the suicides."

"The investigator as he watches the social group is able to observe these breaks appear, increase, multiply, or disappear according as the structure of the collective organism is transformed, according as its vitality is diminished or increased. The psychiatrist concentrates his attention on what is happening in the interior of such a break or gap, and since this is a species of social void or emptiness, it is natural enough that he should explain suicide by the person who commits suicide. The psychiatrist does not see that the real cause of suicide is the social emptiness about the person who commits suicide, and that if there were no such lacunæ in the social structure there would not be any suicides." [15]

Halbwachs elsewhere points out that observation of such social changes must not be taken to imply that the society within which such breakdowns occur is suffering a fatal or final malady. The simpler the community, the more easily does it maintain the integrate character of its activities. The more complex it becomes, the more necessary is it that explicit attention shall be given to the various problems involved in the maintenance of social integrity.

[15] *Les Causes du Suicide*, M. Halbwachs, Felix Alcan, Paris, 1930, p. 448.

There seems to be small doubt that the United States suffers a very considerable degree of the social disorganization diagnosed variously by Shaw, Cavan, and others of the Chicago group.[16] These symptoms do not manifest themselves in Chicago only. Four years ago Dr. J. S. Plant, following some years of experience in Essex County, New Jersey, pointed out to his psychiatric colleagues the danger of a tendency in psychiatry to concentrate attention upon the individual and to neglect the high significance of social changes. His challenge carries the same implications as that of Halbwachs and was published in the *Journal of Psychiatry* a year before the latter's book appeared in Paris. The psychiatrist is ordinarily aware that the "maladjustment" a neurotic suffers is a social maladjustment; he is also aware that this incapacity to get on with other people reflects the early history of such a person, the social void that bred him. But, says Plant, in helping a neurotic, the psychiatrist sometimes forgets to ask whether there is any longer a social order to which the patient may adjust. And, selecting an example of a residential neighborhood not far from New York, Plant proceeds to demonstrate how far the ravages of social disruption have carried. The individual and the family live in temporary quarters, the population of the industrial and of the better residential localities constantly changes. Of one of the better residential areas, he says: "(1) Seventy per cent of the married men have their work so far removed as to mean at least two hours of travelling each day. In some large areas this percentage is ninety. . . . (2) The rapid inroads of apartment life are serving to restrict the size and importance of what we have previously considered

[16] The *anomie* discussed by Durkheim.

the . . . real aspects of the family. (3) Each five years finds slightly over 78 per cent of this population in a new address. This incessant migration is progressing even in areas where as high as 84 per cent of the homes are owned by those who live in them." [17] Plant goes on to point out that in a surrounding such as this, one cannot expect children to grow up with the same sense of social significance and order, with the same capacity of self-control, as children brought up in an environment of greater stability and more obvious collaborate function. Social stratification—the relationship to each other of the various working groups—cannot attain either definition or actuality in a situation where one perhaps lives and moves but certainly has no being. Just as our political and economic studies have for two hundred years tended to take account only of the economic functions involved in living, so also in our actual living we have inadvertently allowed pursuit of economic development to lead us into a condition of extensive social disintegration. As Halbwachs says, the most important problem for a complex and rapidly changing society is the contrivance of means that will assure the preservation of a social integrity of function side by side with the development of function. It is probable that the work a man does represents his most important function in the society; but unless there is some sort of integral social background to his life, he cannot even assign a value to his work. Durkheim's findings in nineteenth-century France would seem to apply to twentieth-century America.

The answer to the question proposed by the research division at Hawthorne—does life in a modern industrial

[17] "Social Factors in Integration," J. S. Plant, *Am. Journal of Psychiatry*, July, 1929.

centre in some way predispose workers to obsessive response—must be tentatively affirmative. What does this tentative affirmative imply? One suspects that the Chicago researches are significant not only for criminal and suicide inquiry, but also significant for students of industrial relations, of psychoneurosis and of education. Beyond this it is evident that any social disorganization on this scale must show itself in a developing instability of economic consumption. Mr. T. W. Lamont remarked some time ago that the United States showed less resistance to the onset of an economic depression than certain older and European countries. It may be that in this there is again a symptom of *anomie*. A community which has been accustomed to a certain manner of living offers resistance to change in proportion as it has held its integrate character. This is true of changes that are beneficial; it is still more true of changes that are the reverse.

The National Committee on Social Changes, appointed by President Hoover, has just issued its report, two large volumes entitled "Social Trends." These volumes have not yet been available for study for a sufficient period of time for adequate comment to be possible. It is nevertheless significant that the committee itself makes an observation to the effect that our social invention has not kept pace with our technical invention. Put in other words, this implies that whereas in the material and scientific spheres we have been careful to develop knowledge and technique, in the human and socio-political we have contented ourselves with haphazard guess and opportunist fumbling. The first requisite is greater knowledge of the type and extent of social change.

Three years ago, the industrial division and the School of Business Administration at Harvard became convinced that study of the human organism at work and rest, important as it is, is not enough; the collaboration of an anthropologist skilled in the use of field techniques was necessary. The Department of Anthropology in Harvard College consented to the appointment of Mr. Lloyd Warner, Assistant Professor of Social Anthropology, to organize the appropriate research. Mr. Warner had recently returned from investigation of a tribe of North Australian blackfellows and set himself to adapt for use in a civilized community the anthropological methods employed to discover primitive social structure and function. He decided to select for study in the first instance a small and typical New England community which bore no obvious trace of rapid or extensive change, which was still sufficiently what it had been in the American historic period. His choice fell upon Newburyport, a small city on the eastern seaboard of Massachusetts, and for two years the study has been in active progress. The work has been done by graduate and undergraduate students of anthropology under Warner's direction; it has been very considerably aided by the intelligent understanding of the citizens themselves. The reports of various inquiries are not yet ready for publication, but something can be said as to the direction in which the findings move.

The situation that has revealed itself in Newburyport is very different from that which seems to be characteristic of the larger city, and especially a larger city like Chicago which exhibits the consequences of rapid and disorderly expansion. The same problems are in some degree manifest; but their proportions are at present manageable. Also they are receiving some attention from citizen committees and are not altogether out of hand. The people who belong to the community live in it and participate in its activities. Many of them have extensive interests elsewhere in the United States; some of them at least occasionally travel and, it may be, far afield. But the outside interest and the travel seem to possess, even in these instances, small power to detach citizens from their essential participation and communal responsibility. It is possible to trace cultural zones in the residential parts of the town and to distinguish between the method of living and the degree of social responsibility which attaches to the different ways of living. But such zones cannot be quartered in square-mile areas upon the city map, nor would arcs of a circle arbitrarily swung outwards from the business centre show much statistical significance. Every citizen knows empirically where such zones begin and end, just as he knows the remoter social implications of the occupancy of a certain type of house in a certain district. But the boundaries of these cultural zones are historically and socially determined; they do not reflect a mathematical consequence of serial losses of control and subsequent deteriorative changes. The typical residents of a particular segregate or class are not so completely ignorant of the other segregates as in a large industrial city. On the contrary, the relation between the three chief cultural groups is carefully organized and is constantly re-organized; the mutual responsibilities involved are defined in an ordered complex of group activities. This city of approximately fifteen thousand inhabitants has rather more than two hundred clubs and associations of varying types. However various these associations, I think it may be claimed that each one organizes its members to some explicit communal responsibility.

The very number of these associations is probably witness to the need for careful attention to the problem of retaining the communal integrity of living under heavy assault from the formless proliferation of the alleged civilization outside. In the third zone of which I have spoken are situated all the foreign "colonies" save one. These colonies all present those problems of "acculturation" which interest the anthropologist in any "culture-contact" situation. In his "Clash of Culture," Pitt-Rivers points out that contact between one culture and another does not necessarily result in benefit. Where one is civilized and the other relatively primitive, the result is more likely to be degradation of both, especially at or near the point of contact.[18] Shaw and Cavan have shown how large a part is played by this phenomenon in the creation of the areas of social disorganization they have investigated. These problems reveal their existence, as I have said, in the smaller Massachusetts community. But they have not grown unheeded to unmanageable size; on the contrary, "community welfare" and other organizations keep pace step by step with the development. Nor are the foreign colonies in so unfavorable a position as elsewhere. Certain of the associations above-named exist to maintain the disciplinary hold of a foreign group upon its members; certain others exist to aid the successful individual to "graduate" into the American community.

The difficulty which attends the study of crime in Chicago, or of symptoms of disorganization elsewhere in our civilization, is the difficulty which attends, for example, the present study of psychopathology. In so far as attention is devoted merely to those areas in which the social controls have broken down, nothing is learned of the nature and development of the social controls them-

[18] "Clash of Culture," Pitt-Rivers, Routledge, 1927, pp. 193 *ff.*

selves; as Halbwachs says, study of a social void can lead to nothing but observation of the disasters which occur in such a void. This is not intended to imply that the researches of Shaw, Cavan, or even Lynd's "Middletown" should not have the interest such work immediately commands; but researches thus directed do need to be balanced by the development of inquiries in other social situations than the pathological.

Another interesting aspect of the Newburyport inquiry is the adaptation of the methods of the anthropological field worker to the investigation of a civilized community. Anthropology at the beginning of its historical development was at first much beset by observers who found only what they had expected to find in studying a primitive community; this tendency is likely to play similar havoc with an attempt by an individual to study his own group, unless he has acquired a skilled technique of investigation. The adaptation of methods which have been developed by functional anthropology in the Andaman Islands, the Trobriands, and Australia would seem to be the only way of assuring adequate and unbiassed observation. This, of course, merely by way of a beginning.

The wisdom of selecting for original study in this manner an as yet undamaged New England community has, I think, become clearly evident. The conclusions that one might otherwise have drawn from studies confined to the disorganized areas of Chicago must be considerably modified. It is evident that even Durkheim's estimate of the dangers of *anomie* (and he had not seen the large American city) is somewhat exaggerated. Human individuals apparently cannot do otherwise than establish and reëstablish social forms or patterns of living. Halbwachs is in this a better guide than Durkheim: "As he watches the social group, the investigator will observe these gaps appear, increase, multiply, or disappear as the structure of the society changes, as its vitality is diminished or increased." [19] The theory of *anomie* is necessary however, if only as a definition of the problem. At any given moment the actuality of *anomie* may present a serious difficulty or even a threat to the continued existence of a particular community: social students must learn to recognize its significant symptoms. But the black spots of disorganization upon the social map of the United States must not yet be interpreted as heralding the downfall of a culture; so much the anthropological study of Newburyport has already shown. These same black spots do nevertheless present a problem in social understanding which calls urgently for attention. Here also, as in the study of neurotic obsession, the more important investigation is perhaps that directed to discovery of the extent of weakened control in relatively stable situations, rather than inquiry confined to situations of extreme disorder. In one aspect of its activities, Newburyport presents a picture of defence, so far successful, against the breakdown of a traditional mode of life. But the defence is empirically devised by citizens and demands the support of research and systematic understanding.

It is not possible to fasten upon industry, or upon any other specified development, the sole responsibility for this problem of social disorganization. Unquestionably a period of exceedingly rapid economic growth has contributed to the disturbance of communal integrity. A subsidiary factor of some importance is the high mobility

[19] *Op. cit.,* p. 448.

of labor in prosperous times in the United States; the immigrant and the foreign colony constitute another. But, in addition to these, defects in the educational system and certain eccentricities of political and economic doctrine have all played some part in the determination of our development to the "top-heaviness" and "lopsidedness" which McDougall claims are symptomatic of "world chaos." [20]

[20] "World Chaos," William McDougall, Covici Friede, 1932, p. 15.

CHAPTER VII

THEORIES OF GOVERNMENT AND THE SOCIAL ORDER

IN this chapter I am attempting to consider briefly certain of the difficulties which civilized governments are facing. I do not mean by this the material problems which in our present circumstance make so urgent a claim on their attention. I mean rather those difficulties which are created for government, whether it be democratic, Fascist, or Bolshevik, by both the official and the popular conception of governmental function. Our knowledge of the actual social function of political authority has not developed equally with our other knowledge. Political theory has tended to relate itself for the most part to its historic origins; it has failed to originate and sustain a vigorous inquiry into the changing structure of society. In the meantime the social context, the actual condition of civilized peoples, has undergone so great a variety of changes that any mere announcement of the ancient formulæ rings hollow and carries no conviction to anyone.

There tends, therefore, to be an unfortunate compulsion upon political debates to move almost invariably in the wrong direction. Let me illustrate by picking up a topic which has for some time and in many countries been made the subject of deafening argument, a topic which refers itself immediately to the pre-revolutionary France of the Physiocrats. Shall industries be govern-

144

ment controlled? If we look backward at the investigations we have been considering—the biochemistry of fatigue, the industrial and social studies of personal equilibrium and "interference"—surely the only observation we can intrude in such political discussions will be that the question who is to control is of small importance as compared with the question whether he is alertly aware of the problems—physiological, personal, social, and technical—involved in a situation both technical and human. The social system of one country expresses itself politically in the form of a monarchy, of another in "democratic individualism," of another in Fascist or Soviet control. Accepting any such condition of a particular situation, one can assert that the industrial problem is otherwise the same for all. The several researches I have reported possess significance equally for a factory on the Volga or for another on the banks of the river Charles.

There is, however, an exceedingly interesting problem in political control which is only rarely discussed and then often by inadvertence. This is the fact, and I think it is unmistakably a fact, that all governments whatever their political type are at present actively increasing their control of industrial and other social functions. This seems to be happening, not only by deliberate intent as in Italy and Russia, but also in England, France, and the United States. In the latter group, politicians struggle against the tendency but are nevertheless forced to yield to it. This movement has its origin, I believe, in two sources, the first of which may be described as an historic misunderstanding; the second is our ignorance and uncontrol of social change. The two are closely interrelated.

(a) The historic misunderstanding. Modern economic theory owes its origin to Quesnay's *"Tableau Economique";* his work was remarkable and is still worthy of the high consideration that continues to be accorded it. Quesnay asserted that certain natural principles would be found to regulate human association in work, once governments had learned to leave industrial development to work out its own destiny. His advice to political authority that it should leave well alone was exceedingly apt with respect to the situation of which he wrote. France of the eighteenth century possessed a vigorous and highly integrate society much hampered in its industrial development by governmental overregulation. The situation, as Quesnay then saw it, showed three aspects which demanded administrative attention: first, a vigorous social organization which given freedom would develop to new powers; second, a political authority which possessed small understanding of the situation, and third, the question thus implied of the relation between the social organism and its political function. It was possible for England of the nineteenth century, tutored by Adam Smith and his successors, to adopt Quesnay's analysis wholeheartedly, because the general description applied sufficiently well to the England of that time. That is to say, the existence of a vigorous and sufficiently integrate English social organism could at that time be assumed. Unfortunately the importance of this assumption as affecting the meaning and truth of Quesnay's doctrine was never clearly stated. John Stuart Mill in his discussion of the limits of the province of government adheres blindly to the political aspect of the physiocratic doctrine. He says: *"Laisser-faire . . .* should be the general practice (*i.e.* of governments): every departure from it,

unless required by some great good, is a certain evil." [1]
Mill failed to see that the truth of Quesnay's statement
is limited to those situations in which the integrity and
health of the social organism can be assumed. Through
the nineteenth century industry developed greater complexity, and popular government was extended by successive stages; finally certain symptoms of the social
anomie of which Durkheim speaks began to manifest
themselves. With the emergence of these symptoms political activities were redoubled, but questions of the
health of the social organism still received no attention.
Thus as other functions of social control diminished or
disappeared and the political function alone survived,
political control again emerged as the sole organ in
actuality of social organization. This was not interpreted
as being the almost invariable symptom of social ill-
health that it historically is; it was welcomed as a liberal
advance. So the doctrine which began by assigning to
political regulation a subsidiary function in social organization, ended by finding it the only available means to
such organization. An unduly abstract political theory
had permitted important social changes to pass un-
noticed.

The misunderstanding was deepened by an attempt to
incorporate the doctrines of Rousseau's social contract
in political theory. This essay probably expressed Rousseau's resentment of the too close control exercised by a
small and highly integrate community over its members.
When he says that man is born free and is everywhere
in chains he is in effect claiming for the individual a right
to the exercise of reason and will, a right to "obey himself alone." He proceeds, however, to extend this individ-

[1] *Polit. Econ.*, Ashley edition, p. 950.

ualism into a political theory which regards a civilized community as a mere horde of persons, a formless anarchy of units upon which a contractual political function alone can impose integrity and order. His doctrine is actually the negative and contrary of all the assumptions of Quesnay's analysis. But English political scientists of the nineteenth century were themselves extreme psychological individualists and consequently found no difficulty in adopting Rousseau's doctrine. So in the nineteenth century the analysis of political ideas, an abstract and unsatisfactory procedure, was substituted for direct social investigation and the development of social understanding was arrested.

(b) Ignorance and uncontrol of social change. Durkheim, towards the end of the nineteenth century, was led by his studies of social disorganization to claim that organization by the State can never be effectively substituted for that voluntary collaboration in work and living which is the symptom of health in a society. When he said this he was considering not the adequacy of any political or social doctrine but the actual course followed by historical civilized development. The successive creation of larger economic units by the coalescence or absorption of smaller units has enabled civilization to give its citizens greater material comfort; it has also, he says, destroyed individual significance in living for the majority of such citizens. "What is in fact characteristic of our historic development is that it has successively destroyed all the ancient social backgrounds. One after another they have been banished either by the slow usury of time or by violent revolution, and in such a fashion that nothing has been developed to replace them." [2] Durk-

[2] *Le Suicide,* Durkheim, Alcan, p. 446.

heim proceeds briefly to trace the historic movement in
this direction up to and including the Revolution. The
France that was left convalescent after the Revolution,
made the discovery, he says, that all the important secondary organization—secondary, that is, to the State—of
its social life had been annihilated (p. 447). He points
out that only a solitary factor of collective organization
had survived the torment—the political state. By the nature of things, since social life must be organized, there
must emerge a tendency for the State to absorb into
itself all organizing activity of a social character. The
long result of our history is therefore that at the point of
its highest culmination the social order is annihilated
and a solitary organizing activity, the political State, is
left facing "a disorganized dust of individuals" (p. 448).
But the State cannot organize effectively; it is central-
ized politically and geographically and consequently is
always too remote morally and spatially to possess anything of the living reality of active collaboration for individuals. This actuality the secondary organizations of a
society used to possess. The State therefore finds its
difficulties of control increase; simultaneously the individual, freed from all intimate social relationship, is
abandoned to a disordered isolation and demoralized.[*]

These views are exaggerated, as we have seen; nevertheless they are interesting as defining one of the major
problems of our time which cannot be successfully at-
tacked by merely political methods. The political method
of the nineteenth century ignored the existence of the
social organism; it was nevertheless possible, for a time,
for political action to aid social development. The same
method cannot succeed when the social organism is itself

[*] *Ibid*, p. 449.

afflicted with an ill which cannot be ignored. There is great need that studies such as that undertaken by the Harvard Anthropological Department at Newburyport shall be immediately multiplied. McDougall, the pioneer in socio-psychological inquiry, has recently published an eloquent appeal for the relation of political and economic study to an anthropological investigation of civilized communities. He says that social science and especially economics cannot be reconstructed except upon a foundation "provided by anthropological research." *

There is, then, an exceedingly interesting problem in political control which does not relate itself in any sense to those present-day discussions which seem to be mere reiteration of *laisser-faire*. It is directly related to an historic failure to study and understand the factors which influence a social culture to development or decay. Political control has become the only social control of which we admit the existence. Ills elsewhere in the social organism reflect themselves immediately in political disequilibrium. Yet such ills cannot be understood or alleviated for so long as their political symptoms alone are studied.

There have been attempts to begin the appropriate studies. Such attempts have usually been handicapped by the inability of the individual to command the collaboration demanded by inquiry upon so large a scale. Or they have been handicapped by the inability of the individual to see that pioneer research work is necessary since the technical methods of science have not yet displaced dialectic from the political field. Some years ago Mr. R. H. Tawney, an English scholar, published an article on "The Sickness of an Acquisitive Society" in

* "World Chaos," McDougall, Covici Friede, 1932, p. 117.

the *Hibbert Journal*. The article aroused such interest that it was republished as a pamphlet by the Fabian Society; finally it was re-written and published as a book.[5] Tawney begins by discussing "rights and functions" and makes very clear the distinction between a functional society in which each individual knows his place and the value of his work to the communal purpose and a disorganized society in which he has the comfort neither of assured work nor of an assured personal value. He shows that in a disorganized society success is measured by the acquisition of wealth rather than by personal responsibility or other criteria of social value. And he proceeds to claim that an extensive "moral change" is cause. "It is not surprising that in the new industrial societies which arose on the ruins of the old régime the dominant note should have been the insistence upon individual rights, irrespective of any social purpose to which their exercise contributed. The economic expansion which concentrated population on the coal measures was, in essence, an immense movement of colonization drifting from the south and east to the north and west; and it was natural that in those regions of England, as in the American settlements, the characteristic philosophy should be that of the pioneer and the mining camp. The change of social quality was profound. But in England, at least, it was gradual, and the 'industrial revolution,' though catastrophic in its effects, was only the visible climax of generations of subtle moral change." [6] Tawney describes this moral change as occurring especially in the relation of religion to social organization. "In the eighteenth century both the State and

---

[5] "The Acquisitive Society," R. H. Tawney, G. Bell & Sons, London. 1921.

[6] *Op. cit.,* p. 10.

the Church had abdicated that part of their sphere which
had consisted in the maintenance of a common body of
social ethics . . ." (p. 12). Later he says, "And the
Church was even more remote from the daily life of mankind than the State. Philanthropy abounded; but religion, once the greatest social force, had become a thing as
private and individual as the estate of the squire or the
working clothes of the labourer" (p. 13).

Two irrelevancies led Tawney away from the interesting task to which he had set his hand. The first is the
idea that morality is a quality which can be developed
personally and then practised socially. In the latter
part of his essay he sets himself not merely to describe
the deterioration of social organization but also to claim
that some person or groups of persons are very much to
blame for these changes. In an apostrophe of the investor
he says: "The *rentier* and his ways, how familiar they
were in England before the war! A public school and
then club life in Oxford and Cambridge, and then another club in town; London in June, when London is
pleasant, the moors in August, and pheasants in October,
Cannes in December and hunting in February and
March; and a whole world of rising bourgeoisie eager to
imitate them, sedulous to make their expensive watches
keep time with this preposterous calendar" (pp. 37, 38).
This is the rhetoric of abuse and has no serious value.
There were, no doubt, those who lived thus before the
war, as after, but the percentage of "Oxford and Cambridge" graduates or of that doubtful class the "rising
bourgeoisie" who sedulously imitated such a scheme of
living was negligible.

Tawney's second irrelevance is his curious belief that
morality and religion are something more than specified

aspects of a social life and organization. Morality, for example, is a word we use to describe the actualities of personal inter-relation involved in an ordered scheme of living. When Tawney refers to the industrial colonizing movement in eighteenth-century England "from south and east to north and west," it does not occur to him to ask whether the change of occupation and the extensive movement away from former settlements may not have contributed something to the disturbance of ordered personal inter-relationship and so to the "moral change" he specifies. It seems that he is affected by the Rousseau method of arguing from the individual to the society. Actually the problem *is not that of the sickness of an acquisitive society; it is that of the acquisitiveness of a sick society.* The acquisitiveness he selects for such unsparing condemnation is itself no more than a symptom of the failing integration which invariably accompanies too rapid social change.

A few weeks ago a magazine article upon our present discontents made use of this distinction between a functional and an acquisitive society; Russia and Denmark, it was said, possess a "functional economy," America and England an "acquisitive economy." This statement may, of course, be merely a "witch-hunt" to sheet home the blame for evil magic to some person or persons. This is perennially comforting to human beings, even the civilized, and in this event I have no comment to offer. But the assertion about Russia, if seriously intended, is exceedingly doubtful. At present Russia is immensely preoccupied with material development, and rightly. In an effort to rouse peasant and worker to a sense of social responsibility of larger scale, she is moving peasants and workers from place to place and violently disrupting all their historic and cultural personal inter-relationships. This is probably necessary and may perhaps be accomplished without significant disorganization. But from the point of view of social study, the road Russia is travelling is very like the road that England and America have travelled. And there is no evidence that her high authorities understand, any better than we did, the need of anthropological in addition to economic research.

If we are really desirous of studying a functional society, we must have recourse to the investigations of the anthropologists. Such studies show that in a primitive community the logic of personal inter-relation in work and living operates much more systematically than with us. In such a society every tool or weapon, every ritual performance or magic and the whole kinship system is inexorably related to communal activity and function. Malinowski has based his "functional anthropology" upon his studies of the Trobriand islanders in the Western Pacific.[7] There he discovered a curious, to our way of thinking, economic system of inter-island exchange of commodities by gift. He describes the magical ceremonies to assure success devised for every step of the exchange procedure; the ceremonies begin with the selection and cutting down of a tree to make a canoe and end only with the ritual presentation of the goods. The part each individual plays in work and ceremony marks his communal participation. The life of a Trobriander is almost completely constituted of social rituals which have either an economic function or determine otherwise the details of his social living. A. R. Brown has made similar studies of the Andaman islanders and of Australian aborigines. In West Australia "when a stranger comes to a camp

[7] "Argonauts of the Western Pacific," B. Malinowski.

that he has never visited before, he does not enter the camp, but remains at some distance. A few of the older men after a while approach him, and the first thing they proceed to do is to find out who the stranger is. . . . The discussion proceeds on genealogical lines until all parties are satisfied of the exact relation of the stranger to each of the natives present in the camp. When this point is reached, the stranger can be admitted to the camp. . . ." [8] Perhaps these illustrations will suffice to show briefly how close is the organization of a primitive community to its various functions. The stranger's kinship, in Brown's description, defined his social relationships; his economic and other functions could be immediately deduced from his place in the structural kinship scheme. My colleague Warner has shown me tabulated records of Australian kinship that resemble complex geometrical patterns. Yet no written record of such a scheme is either possible for the tribe itself or needed by it. Members of the group live so completely in the scheme and by it that they do not need to remember it; it has become the inevitable *gestalt* in terms of which they understand everything—to which they refer every experience for interpretation.

There is an interesting observation to be made here, which Tawney does not introduce into his discussion of a functional society. In these primitive communities there is room for an individual to develop skill, but there is no latitude for the development of radical or intelligent opinions. If he develops special prowess in hunting or war he gains *mana* and reputation; but he is not expected to develop any intelligent thinking about the de-

[8] "The Tribes of Western Australia," A. R. Brown, *Journal Anthropological Institute*, 1913, p. 152.

tails of social organization. The unit is, in a sense, the group or commune, and not the separate individuals; the development of anything in the nature of personal capacity must be subordinate to the whole. With us it is quite otherwise; the intent of education in a complex society is to develop intelligence and independence of judgment in the individual. The primitive community develops a social intelligence and not individual intelligences. Over almost the entire area of a man's life the society thinks for him; and he learns only the social responses he must produce in reply to given signals. This is a very restricted method of living, but it is highly integrate and "functional"; in addition to this it is very comfortable for the individual, who does not need to "wrestle with a solitary problem."

Now I have no doubt that when Harvard and other anthropological studies of the United States are further developed, we shall find that even a civilized society is unable completely to dispense with this form of intelligent social direction of individual activities. Our educational systems are elaborated as if intended to develop intelligent and independent judgment over the whole system of individual living; but educational authorities have to recognize that the total number of persons who can even approximate to this ideal is very small, and that even these few, by reason of the demands of their special studies upon their time and energy, are compelled to accept the judgment of society in most matters. The advantage of education is that it gives the individual a technique of inquiry such that he is able to re-order his thought and action in any direction, if revision should become necessary; for the rest, most of us must live, more or less, by the social code. Since such dependence or independence of judgment as we possess is derived from social training and education, a question as to the method of its derivation becomes important.

Many years ago William James described the world of the baby's earliest observation as presenting to the baby one "big, blooming, buzzing confusion." Whether this is actually so or not, the statement has a sufficient logical relevance; the baby is unable to identify anything except as the stimulus of unconditioned or recently conditioned response. He has to learn to select, from amongst the multiple items that offer, those stimuli or objects which, in some functional way, possess significance for him. In all his years of learning, the infant is immensely aided in the establishment of necessary discriminations by the social milieu into which he is born. No one who has any acquaintance with the personal habits of neglected babies can fail to recognize the unrealized gifts of control and response conferred upon the infant from his earliest weeks by an ordered social surrounding.

Thus the reality of the infant's first knowledge is already a socio-reality. That is to say, his reality is informed and ordered by social conditioning to such an extent that for the rest of his life he is usually unable to complete his escape from the social interpretations thus imposed upon him. Only by the most arduous experimental study and logical elaboration can he win clear and socially untrammelled understanding. It is customary in these days to conceive social dependence as wholly disadvantage. This condemnation neglects the fact that the child and adolescent greatly need social support and sanction during the entire period of tutelage. Without such tutelage and support the individual cannot achieve clear vision and knowledge. Alternative there is none:

psychopathology has shown that infants unfortunately deprived of this social guidance grow up, the variants of circumstance, to psychoneurosis or crime.

Nevertheless the doctrines of psychoanalysis with respect to the development of the childish mentality cannot be accepted for the following reasons:

(a) These doctrines are not based upon actual studies of children but upon inferences from the pre-occupations of morbid adults or adolescents. Anna Freud herself admits that the "analytic" procedures cannot properly be applied to children.[*]

(b) Halbwach's criticism, quoted above, is that the mental disability of the psychoneurotic adult is due to the fact that he has lived in a "social void." The whole of psychoanalytic literature is itself evidence of the part played by a defective infantile surrounding in the determination to psychoneurosis. The psychoneurotic is therefore singularly ill-chosen as a sample of the characteristic mental events in a normal childish up-bringing.

(c) The concealed assumption of the doctrine of original sin invalidates the psychoanalytic findings. The theory that life is a strenuous fight to subdue perversion, that the human mind is by nature "pathogenic" (*i.e.* predisposed to the pathological) is not a possible starting point for biological observation.

It is sometimes said that observation of the psychoneurotic struggle for serenity throws much light upon the mental processes of the normal. Bleuler's caution needs

[*] Technic of Child Analysis, Nervous and Mental Monographs, No. 48, 1928, pp. 56 *ff.*

to be applied here, the caution namely that although the mental processes of an ordinarily healthy person are in some respects like those of a psychoneurotic, one must always remember that such a person is not a psychoneurotic. It is not the resemblance but the difference between the normal person and the psychoneurotic which demands definition.

The most interesting study of the method by which the child simultaneously develops his social adjustments and a capacity for logical thinking is unquestionably that of Jean Piaget of the Rousseau Institute and the University of Geneva. Piaget is a biologist and was formerly an authority on molluscs. His observation of the child is consequently an adaptation of biological procedure. He regards the human infant as a superior kind of mollusc, endowed with biologically unusual powers of comprehension of, and adaptation to, other molluscs. He gives full consideration to the observations of psychologists, psychopathologists, and anthropologists; but the categories or classifications which he uses himself in the first instance are very simply descriptive. For Piaget the human being, like the mollusc, is active or passive during the twenty-four hours of the day; these activities or passivities must be studied as functions that serve the organism. The human being is biologically unique in respect of his capacity for conserving and developing the conditioning effect upon him of his surroundings; in consequence of this capacity human functions are not identical at four years and at forty. However apparent the identity of mental methods at different ages it must be distrusted; the organism's developed powers must be studied in relation to the stage of its development.

The method Piaget first employed—he developed

other methods later—was that of direct observation. Observers were appointed to select and follow each a particular child for a month at the morning class of the *Maison des Petits* at Geneva. The child's actions and attitudes were closely watched; everything said was written down "in minute detail and in its context." [10] Piaget's first book reports the findings of this method with respect to two small boys, special attention being given to their various spontaneous utterances and to the circumstances in which the comments were made. It was at once observed that a child's speech is by no means always addressed to other persons in the immediate vicinity. On the contrary, a large proportion of the recorded utterances are of the nature of soliloquy, reflective comments on what the child is doing or on what is happening about him. The various speeches of the two subjects are therefore classified in two general categories, soliloquy speech and social speech. The soliloquies are sometimes socially stimulated or provoked ("repetition" and "collective monologue") but are not socially addressed to another person; they are rather of the nature of monologue [11] and, although he does not realize it, are addressed by the individual to himself. [12] Upon the basis of such observations Piaget proceeds to consideration of the difference between "egocentric" soliloquy and "socialized" speech. This distinction becomes one of the main foundations of his work.

The word "egocentricity," as Piaget uses it, must not be confused with our ordinary use of the adjective "self-centred" as applied to description of an adult. Piaget strongly repudiates the psychoanalytic concept of "nar-

[10] 'The Language and Thought of the Child," Jean Piaget, Harcourt, Brace & Co., 1927, p. 5.
[11] *Ibid.*, p. 9. [12] *Ibid.*, p. 14.

cissism" as an adequate description of infantile egocentricity for the very reason that it manifests this confusion.[13] The child, up to the age of about seven years,
cannot think about himself in any adult sense, because
he has not elaborated sufficiently the distinction between
himself and the external world or the distinction between
his thought and things—for him there is no difference
between logical and causal relation.[14] It is the inability
to discriminate these differences which makes the child's
thinking egocentric in the Piaget sense; it is as if his
organism were continuous with the external world, with
no clear "cut-off" at the organic periphery. He cannot
think of himself as clearly distinct from other people and
things; so also in thinking of things he is unable to be
impersonal and objective, to distinguish them clearly
from himself. A baby is as interested in his own hand
and finger movements as in something the hand is hold-
ing; he is indifferent to fine shades of the classification
"me" and "not-me." One might perhaps generalize here
by saying that the meanings a child gives to objects in
the world about him are all meanings in terms of their
use or other immediate relation to himself. This is, of
course, an insufficient and oversimplified statement because it takes no account of the special character of
childish logic.

In his first volume Piaget had made use of Bleuler's
(and Janet's) distinction between two kinds of thinking
—active or directed thinking and passive or undirected
thinking.[15] Directed thought is conscious of its aim, intelligent, adapted to reality, true or false, and com-

[13] "The Child's Conception of the World," J. Piaget, Harcourt,
Brace & Co., 1929, p. 151.
[14] "The Child's Conception of the World," French edition, Alcan,
pp. 146 and 156.
[15] "Language and Thought," p. 43.

municable by language. Undirected thought is unaware of its aims, not adapted to reality, imaginative, does not critically establish truths but establishes relations and remains essentially incommunicable. In the adult the former has become concentration, the latter reflection, but it is a mistake to suppose that the child can either concentrate or reflect as the adult does. Since educational systems at present concern themselves mainly with fact and logic, they usually do little directly to help the individual to establish control of his thinking. In instances where an individual has not established such control it is his reflective thinking which, in effect, is out of hand. He feels that his reflections are uncontrolled, obsessive, or compulsive, the "undirected" character has become positive rather than merely passive.[16] There is therefore a right relation between active thinking—sustained attention—and passive thinking—revery—in the normal adult; by active thinking we learn to discriminate, by passive thinking we unify. our experiences and reconsider our active discriminations. Piaget in his second volume quotes this observation of Janet's and points out that the childish revery serves to unify the child's thinking although in a manner quite unlike that of an adult and ordered logic.[17] In the introduction to the third volume he says: "The thought of the child approximates more nearly to a totality of attitudes issuing at once from action and revery than to the thought, conscious of itself and systematic, of the adult."[18] The child does not "think" in the adult sense, his mental life

[16] *Les Névroses*, Janet, Flammarion, pp. 350 *ff*.
[17] "Judgment and Reasoning in the Child," Harcourt, Brace & Co., 1928, p. 204.
[18] "The Child's Conception of the World," French edition, Introduction, p. 35.

is rather to be described as an alternation of action and revery—the revery occurring as a species of "running comment" on action. "Egocentric" thinking proceeds immediately to synthesis; things that co-exist in fact are reported uncritically as totalities. Almost any sort of connection is thus accepted and justified, without any thought of chance association.[19] The identification of totalities and some sort of response must precede the development of controlled reflection, of skill, and of graduated response.

One of the most interesting observations that is reported variously in all five of Piaget's published volumes is that the development of logical capacity proceeds step by step with the socialization of the child's thought. It is known that an adult of insufficient social experience will not be merely socially maladjusted; he will also be found to be using inferior logical techniques. Piaget makes it evident that a child has to acquire a capacity for making the responses socially appropriate to different situations before he can possibly understand either the responses or the situations. His first achieved code of social behavior is therefore somewhat suggestive of Pavlov's "signal reflexes." His responses are not, of course, mere reflexes, but they nevertheless are responses to signals rather than to situations. It is only as his social experience accumulates and his logical formulations are elaborated that he can possibly develop reasoned comprehension and independent judgment. But he cannot achieve this unless he continues to live in a sufficiently ordered and sufficiently stable society. The psychoanalysts have wisely observed the far-reaching effect of a disordered social and family environment upon a child's

[19] "Language and Thought," p. 185.

temperamental stability and happiness. Piaget's inquiries enable us to gain some understanding of the mental privations such an infancy implies.

Piaget's researches seem to indicate that even in a civilized community with an elaborate educational system the individual must pass through a stage in which he develops appropriate and ordered responses to social signals without any real capacity to understand or judge social situations. Understanding and adequate judgment are acquired late and by many people are not acquired at all, except within some limited area of achieved skill and logic. Generally speaking, therefore, the responses of any adult individual to his surrounding are of three types:

> (a) Logical. In this area he has developed skill and capacity for discrimination and independent judgment.
> (b) Non-logical. This type of response is described above as "signal response." The individual's actions may be adequate to the situation, but any intelligence they exhibit is socially and not personally derived. This form of response is the effect of training in a social code of behavior.
> (c) Irrational. Non-logical response is typical of social adjustment. Irrational response, on the other hand, is symptomatic of social maladjustment and shows all the signs of obsession. Both types of response are rooted in individual unreason, but it is only the latter which technically interests the psychopathologist.

The non-logical response, that, namely, which is in strict conformity with a social code, makes for social order and discipline, *for effective collaboration in a restricted range of activity,* and for happiness and a sense of security in the individual. It is specially characteristic of primitive societies and of small and undeveloped communities. This concentration of intelligence and decision in the group rather than the individual works exceedingly well, provided that the group does not have to face too many novel problems simultaneously, provided that it is not forced into a cultural clash with another group.

The irrational response—the sign of obsessive and personal maladjustment—is not characteristic merely of individuals who have been brought up in a "social void." It appears also in any situation that is "anomique" in Durkheim's phrase. That is to say, when a code or tradition, that has been sufficiently adequate to its material problems and to its social controls, is faced with a situation that it cannot meet, the individuals of the group will turn from non-logical to irrational action. They will lose their capacity for disciplined coöperation. This serves to complicate the problem further and may in extreme cases break the society.

Here, then, is a curiosity of the modern situation. If a specialist group develops scientific knowledge and applies it to technical practice at too high a speed for general social adjustment to the change, one effect is to transform non-logical social organization into irrational social disorganization. This is especially true where the technical practice affects a group that is not party to the scientific knowledge. For example, engineering innovations have had a more disorganizing effect upon industry than biochemical discoveries upon medicine. My colleague Warner has pointed out that industrial methods have been rapidly developed of late years in a logical or scientific direction, and internationally rather than nationally. The consequence is that the imposition of highly systematized industrial procedures upon all the civilized cultures has brought to relative annihilation the cultural traditions of work and craftsmanship. Simultaneously the development of a high labor mobility and a clash of cultures has seriously damaged the traditional routine of intimate and family life in the United States. Generally the effect has been to induce everywhere a considerable degree of social disorganization; the comfortable non-logic of every social code has been reduced, at least in part, to irrational exasperation—without any prospect of development towards better understanding for the average citizen. It would seem that one of the important problems discovered by the research division at Hawthorne—the failure of workers and supervisors to understand their work and working conditions, the widespread sense of personal futility—is general to the civilized world and not merely characteristic of Chicago. The belief of the individual in his social function and solidarity with the group—his capacity for collaboration in work —these are disappearing, destroyed in part by rapid scientific and technical advance. With this belief his sense of security and of well-being also vanishes and he begins to manifest those exaggerated demands of life which Durkheim has described. "The stability and social health of any community, whether a tribe or a nation, however high or low in the scale of culture or complexity, may be reckoned by the degree of integration or disintegration it exhibits, and . . . every weakening of the tribal tie destroys the social purpose of each member of it." [20]

[20] "Human Biology," G. H. Pitt-Rivers, Vol. IV, No. 2, May, 1932, p. 250.

No form of political action can ever substitute for this loss. Political action in a given community presumes the desire and capacity of individuals to work together; the political function cannot operate in a community from which this capacity has disappeared.

CHAPTER VIII

THE PROBLEM OF THE ADMINISTRATOR

THERE has been much human investigation in industry, or undertaken in connection with industry, which I have not reported. The findings of vocational selection and guidance, the development of tests of intelligent capacity, physiological studies of the relation of diet or physique or posture to work and activity—all these inquiries are important and of established significance. To cover so wide a field in eight chapters would, however, be impossible. The selection of certain researches for report is justified not merely by the fact that the studies described are all represented at present in Harvard University in a collaborative undertaking; the selection is justified also in two other ways. The first is that these various studies—biochemical, medical, industrial, anthropological—show signs of developing a coherent unity of relation which, if it continues to advance, will greatly increase our understanding and control of the human problems of an industrial civilization. The second is that the problems studied possess a peculiar interest and urgency in the present situation of world affairs. They are, in fact, the problems the conditions of which we know least well, the human issues which are in most serious need of skilled attention. The tentative findings I have reported may be briefly summarized as follows:

There is not a single simple form of organic fatigue;

168

there are many fatigues. The fatigues so far studied
by physiologists are identifiable organic disabilities due
to:

> (a) a defective capacity in the individual. For
> example, he is "out of training" for running.
>
> (b) some external condition which "interferes" to
> make continuance of work impossible. For example,
> an external temperature of 95° F. with insufficient
> air movement.

The fatigue disabilities studied are rapidly cumulative
in effect; once manifest, they speedily stop the exercise
or performance. The alternative to such disabilities is
the achievement of a "steady state," a condition of
equilibrium or stability which permits the almost indefinite continuance of the activity. Studies of the performances of men or of the laboratory dogs while in this
"steady state" give no present support to the business-
economic theory of a fatigue, gradual in onset, which is
related to the depletion of fuel reserves.

Industrial studies of "interferences" other than organic, and of work activities other than those which call
for gross muscular exertion, lead to similar conclusions.
These studies, whether conducted in England or in the
United States, indicate that words such as "monotony"
or "boredom" find no simple equivalent in fact; individual differences and differences of personal and social
situations must be closely assessed. Even in the earliest
work of Vernon and Wyatt it was discovered that "temperamental" and social factors are as important as differences of type of work or of intelligent capacity. May
Smith's statement that the repetition work is "a thread
of the total pattern but is not the total pattern" provides

a phrase generally descriptive of the findings of this method of inquiry. As the long industrial day wears through, the repetition work remains the same considered as a mere performance. But as an aspect of a human situation it does not remain the same; organic interferences such as hunger, mental hazards involved in the changing inter-personal situation appear as new variables which may shift the general equilibrium and so find reflection in the output records of the work.

The Western Electric Company in a series of industrial studies over a period of more than five years makes essentially comparable discoveries. The output of the five girl workers in the "test room" continues a slow advance for a period of three years and finally steadies at a record "high." This major gain in its upward passage ignores the experimental changes arbitrarily introduced from time to time by the officers of the research division. The girls themselves are frankly puzzled by the improvement, but attribute the change to something which they cannot clearly specify, something of the nature of a freedom from constraints or "interferences" which operate in the departments outside the "test room." They show a more stable equilibrium or greater resistance to adverse circumstance than workers in a less advantageous situation; it is experimentally demonstrated that an apparent return to the original conditions of work has no significant consequence for the output curve or for the group morale. An equivalent experiment in the department outside the "test room" results in loss of morale and diminished output when a privilege is withdrawn.

The Company extends the experiment by instituting an interview programme to discover the nature of the "interferences" or constraints from which the experimental room is free. Twenty thousand persons are interviewed in two and one-half years and the inquiry goes through several stages:

(a) At first it is essentially industrial and is especially designed to discover whether "interferences" or constraints experienced by workers are related to defective methods of supervision.

(b) The study is temporarily baffled by an apparent finding that statements in interviews about persons are not sufficiently reliable to be made the basis for changes in executive policy. This leads to a study of various psychological theories of the interview, and to an attempt to relate distortions or exaggerations to the personal histories and personal contexts involved in such statements. In this phase the inquiry tends to minimize somewhat the rôle of the external and social situation and to intensify the psychological and analytic investigation of the person. As a by-product, however, a reliable technique of interviewing and a few capable interviewers are discovered.

(c) In the third phase it is realized that the very anonymity of the interviews though it may yield knowledge of personal contexts yet deprives the research of the possibility of relating statements to their actual industrial context; that is, to the actualities of a particular industrial situation. A final innovation of method seeks accordingly to study the individuals of a working group simultaneously by interview and by direct observation. Observation of the events of a day or week in a particular department and of the changing social inter-relation provides a context in the light of which many statements made by individuals of the group in interview may be interpreted and understood.

In the final phase of the Hawthorne inquiry it thus became possible to specify the area in which constraint and the sense of personal futility were manifest; to some extent the sources of such constraint and the freedom achieved in the "test rooms" could be understood.

The industrial inquiry nevertheless makes clear that the problems of human equilibrium and effort are not completely contained within the area controlled by factory organization and executive policy. Certain of the sources of personal disequilibrium, and especially the low resistance to adverse happenings in the ordinary workroom, must be attributed to the developing social disorganization and consequent *anomie* which is in these days typical of living conditions in or near any great industrial centre. This developing *anomie* has changed the essential nature of every administrative problem— whether governmental or industrial. It is no longer possible for an administrator to concern himself narrowly with his special function and to assume that the controls established by a vigorous social code will continue to operate in other areas of human life and action. All social controls of this type have weakened or disappeared —this being symptomatic of the diminished integrity of the social organism. The existing situation, both within the national boundaries and as between nations, demands therefore that special attention be given to restatement of the problem of administration as the most urgent issue of the present.

This aspect of civilized development found clear statement some years ago, in 1913, by Brooks Adams. "Social consolidation is . . . not a simple problem, for social consolidation implies an equivalent capacity for administration. I take it to be an axiom that perfection in administration must be commensurate to the bulk and momentum of the mass to be administered, otherwise the centrifugal will overcome the centripetal force, and the mass will disintegrate. In other words, civilization would dissolve. It is in dealing with administration, as I apprehend, that civilizations have usually, though not always, broken down, for it has been on administrative difficulties that revolutions have for the most part supervened. Advances in administration seem to presuppose the evolution of new governing classes, since, apparently, no established type of mind can adapt itself to changes in environment, even in slow-moving civilizations, as fast as environments change. Thus a moment arrives when the minds of any given dominant type fail to meet the demands made upon them, and are superseded by a younger type, which is in turn set aside by another still younger, until the limit of the administrative genius of that particular race has been reached. Then disintegration sets in, the social momentum is gradually relaxed, and society sinks back to a level at which it can cohere. To us, however, the most distressing aspect of the situation is that the social acceleration is progressive in proportion to the activity of the scientific mind which makes mechanical discoveries, and it is therefore a triumphant science which produces those ever more rapidly recurring changes in environment to which men must adapt themselves at their peril. As, under the stimulant of modern science, the old types (*i.e.* of administrators) fail to sustain themselves, new types have to be equally rapidly evolved. . . ." [1] Brooks Adams proceeds to observe that under modern conditions the "rapidity of intellectual mutation is without precedent" and the possibility of maintaining administrative quality, and, by consequence, stability of social equilibrium, gravely in doubt.

Pareto, the eminent Italian author of the only treatise on general sociology, discusses the importance of high quality in the administrative group in relation to the maintenance of social equilibrium. He observes that leadership in any society vests in two types of *élite*—the governmental and the non-governmental, the latter including the direction of all industrial and economic activities. In Europe these administrative leaders have, historically speaking, constituted an aristocracy. He says: "Aristocracies do not last. Whatever the cause, the fact is incontestable that after a certain time they disappear. History is a graveyard of aristocracies." [2] He continues by pointing out, as Brooks Adams has done, that in any vigorous society there is a continual and necessary movement upwards of capable persons and families from a lower class. These new arrivals by their quality and energy revivify and maintain the general administrative capacity. [3] If anything occurs to interrupt this social mobility—the downward movement of the effete, the upward movement of the vigorous and capable—then the failure to maintain a "circulation of the *élite*" will find reflection in disturbances of social equilibrium. [4]

Now it is not possible to say, as a result of direct and careful observation, that we are at present suffering the effects of a failure to maintain a "circulation of the *élite*."

[1] "The Theory of Social Revolutions," Brooks Adams, The Macmillan Co., pp. 204-5.
[2] *Traité de Sociologie Générale*, Vilfredo Pareto, French edition, Vol. II, chap. xi, p. 1306.
[3] *Ibid.*, paragraph 2054.   [4] Paragraphs 2055-6.

It must, however, be confessed that leaders of society the world over have shown very little perspicacity or foresight in the present serious crisis. It is "as if" the necessary "circulation" of administrators of which Pareto speaks had been interrupted. Brooks Adams, writing in 1913, prophesied the advent of just such a crisis. He points out that a modern society can hope to maintain a stable equilibrium in the midst of rapid change only by ensuring that it has amongst its administrators (of both types—governmental and non-governmental), a sufficient number who possess "a high order of generalizing mind —a mind which can grasp a multitude of complex relations." "But," he adds, "this is a mind which can, at best, only be produced in small quantity and at high cost." [5] He proceeds to claim that our educational system has not sufficiently raised its standards "save in science and mechanics, and the relative overstimulation of the scientific mind has now become an actual menace to order because of the inferiority of the administrative intelligence." That is to say, we are suffering from what McDougall has described as "lopsidedness" in the development of an *élite*. We have developed scientific research and the training of scientists admirably; we have failed utterly to promote any equivalent educational development directed to the discovery and training of administrators of exceptional capacity. These considerations led Brooks Adams to infer that "the extreme complexity of the administrative problems presented by modern industrial civilization" was "beyond the compass" of the mentality of the administrators of his time. "If this be so," he adds, "American society as at present organized . . . can concentrate no further and, as nothing in the universe

[5] *Op. cit.*, p. 217.

is at rest, if it does not concentrate, it must probably begin to disintegrate. Indeed we may perceive incipient signs of disintegration all about us. . . ." [6] Who shall say that this prophecy, made twenty years ago, has not found some fulfilment in the present crisis?

The problem that we face does not, however, reflect the historic European problem of barriers, artificially created, to the passage upwards in society of an *élite*. I believe that the United States, in spite of its present social and administrative difficulties, is fortunately placed in this regard. The problem is rather that of a failure to specify sufficiently clearly the questions which most urgently require an answer. Having made such an assertion, I can easily imagine an indignant retort to the effect that the important questions have been fully stated. Listening carefully, we should no doubt hear faint echoes of such phrases as "gold standard," "inflation," "price level," "tariffs," "technological advance"—still farther off a fainter European echo which sounds like "debts." If we turn from these phrases to the considered statements of our leaders, we find President Hoover at the Lincoln memorial dinner claiming that the prerequisite to the settlement of these subsidiary questions is "the restoration of confidence." On the other side of the Atlantic, Sir Arthur Salter declares that no problem will find resolution until we can devise means of diminishing that fatal "economic nationalism" which at present bars every road to happier circumstance. In the view of these high authorities, then, the primary difficulty is a human complication of the mechanical and economic; the latter indeed, the mechanical and economic, apart from the human complication present no serious

[6] *Op. cit.,* pp. 226-7.

problem at all. But "confidence" and "economic nationalism" are merely phrases; they indicate, it is true, but
they do not describe or explain. We are faced with the
fact, then, that in the important domain of human understanding and control we are ignorant of the facts and
their nature; our opportunism in administration and
social inquiry has left us incapable of anything but im-
potent inspection of a cumulative disaster. We do not
lack an able administrative *élite,* but the *élite* of the
several civilized powers is at present insufficiently posted
in the biological and social facts involved in social organization and control. So we are compelled to wait for the
social organism to recover or perish without adequate
medical aid.

The problems specified by President Hoover and Sir
Arthur Salter—the solution of which is prerequisite to
recovery—are problems of human collaboration. When,
within the national group, men begin to work together for
a common end, confidence will be restored. Similarly
with the international situation as between the various
national units, "economic nationalism" is but a sign
of failure to state the complexity of the human factors
contained in the problem of working together. To the
better definition of this problem, the various researches
I have reported contribute the first pale gleams of
illumination.

The first problem is that of the failure of collaborate
effort within the nation. This failure, considered as a
symptom of social disorganization, is far more significant
than the emergence of black spots of crime or suicide
upon the social geography. It is illustrated in the developed misunderstanding between employers and workers
in every civilized country; this has persisted for a century

without any sign of amelioration. It is, however, only the name of the problem which has persisted; the problem itself has, I think, completely changed its form since, for example, the England of 1832. At that time, as the Hammonds show, it was essentially a problem of wages and working conditions; long hours of work and low wages were the rule.' Since then wages have risen considerably, the conditions of work have much improved; the worker's standards of consumption are higher, he has established for his children a right to education and to freedom from the worse forms of exploitation. Communist Russia has not yet been able to establish, in respect of real wages and satisfactory working conditions, an equivalence with the countries she calls "capitalist." This is not fair criticism, but merely passing comment; the new Russia is too newly born for her achievements to be assessed. The idea that Russia will necessarily do better by her workers in the future, immediate or remote, than we do by ours is, however, equally unwarranted. For the moment she is obsessed, as we are, with the need of developing better methods for the discovery of an administrative *élite*, better methods of maintaining working morale. If the actualities of the situation be considered, and mere words such as capitalism and Bolshevism for the moment set aside, then it must be admitted that the present problems of Russia, on her own confession, are remarkably like the present problems of Detroit.

Better methods for the discovery of an administrative *élite*, better methods of maintaining working morale. The country that first solves these problems will infallibly outstrip the others in the race for stability, security, and

' "The Town Labourer: 1760-1832," J. L. and Barbara Hammond.

development. There is one important aspect of the em-
ployer-employee problem which has persisted through a
century of change in industrial organization, in wages
and in working conditions. This is the problem which
was tentatively stated in the final phases of the interview
study at Hawthorne. It may be briefly expressed in a
claim that at no time since the industrial revolution has
there been, except sporadically here and there, anything
of the nature of effective and whole-hearted collaboration
between the administrative and the working groups in
industry. To "take sides" immediately on an issue such
as this and to assign heavy blame to one side or other
is useless. The failure is due to our incapacity to define
the actual problem with sufficient precision. And until
such definition is attempted, public discussion of the
issues will do little except to load upon an already com-
plicated situation an added burden of mutual suspicion
and distrust. Such a method of procedure can only make
the existing difficulties more acute, and the solution more
unlikely. Dispassioned understanding, for us as for
Russia, is the greatest need.

These problems for a century have been defined in
terms of economics and the clear logic of economics; social and human factors have been disregarded. If we seek
to know more of the part played by such factors, the
simplest situation that we can first inspect is the collaboration in work which has been studied in primitive
peoples by anthropologists—Malinowski, A. R. Brown,
Lloyd Warner. Amongst the Australian aborigines their
method of living involves an almost perfect collaboration drilled into members of the tribe in such a fashion
that a kinship relation, a social ceremony, an economic
duty become signals or commands to act or respond in a

certain manner. I say "drilled into" members of a tribe, because although individual actions, as with a regiment of soldiers, are intelligently related to the actions of others and to the situation, yet no member of the tribe can expound the system and its grounds as a logic. The tribe responds to situations as a unit; each member knows his place and part although he cannot explain it. The analogy with military discipline and drill must not, of course, be pushed to an extreme; primitive collaboration is rather the effect in action of a primitive social code. From the point of view of its simple effectiveness, however, it is more like a "drilled" and military evolution than like our civilized inter-relationships.

A century of scientific development, the emergence of a considerable degree of social disorganization—these and certain effects of education have led us to forget how necessary this type of non-logical social action is to achievement and satisfaction in living. Before the present era, changes in method of living tended to come gradually, usually there was no sudden disruption of slowly evolved methods of working together. Even now one can witness in Europe the successful accomplishment of a necessary economic duty as a purely social function, comparable with the ritual performances of a primitive tribe. The vintage activities and ceremonies of the French peasantry, for example, in the Burgundy district present features essentially similar to the activities of the primitive, although at a higher level of understanding and skill. In the United States we have travelled rapidly and carelessly from this type of simple social and economic organization to a form of industrial organization which assumes that every participant will be a devotee of systematic economics and a rigid logic. This unthinking assumption does not "work" with us, it does not "work" in Russia; it has never "worked" in the whole course of human history. The industrial worker, whether capable of it or no, does not want to develop a blackboard logic which shall guide his method of life and work. What he wants is more nearly described as, first, a method of living in social relationship with other people and, second, as part of this an economic function for and value to the group. The whole of this most important aspect of human nature we have recklessly disregarded in our "triumphant" industrial progress.

In England, trade unionism no doubt came into being as a necessary defence of working class interests. But it developed for a time as an attempt to adapt and modernize social organization and the social code. As the tempo of industrial development became faster and the scientist and engineer—logicians both—established their grip of industrial procedures the possibility of comprehension, or any element of control, by workers in the mass receded infinitely. The trade union thus came to represent in many localities the very essence of conservative reaction—the resistance of a dying social code to innovation. There was nowhere amongst the administrative group a sufficient appreciation of the human values contained in a social code of behavior; so the battle between an attempt to conserve human values and economic innovation developed.

In the United States changes finally came with such rapidity that any attempt to save the non-logic of collaboration became futile. It was as if one were to drill a regiment with a new set of commands and a new drill book every day. The result was not discipline and collaboration but disorder and resistance. The rapid pace of industrial development, uninformed by human research or knowledge, dispersed the last possibilities of collaborate and social effort and imposed upon the workers a low level of human organization from which social participation and social function were excluded. This low-level organization, like trade unionism, also represents a conservative and reactionary attempt to conserve human values; its chief symptom is "stalling," a procedure apparently resented as much by the workers themselves as by management. Since this seems to be as characteristic of Russia as of the United States, it is probable that the human problems involved are fundamental and contain no "political" element. Again it may be said that the question is not who is to control, but rather a question as to what researches are essential to the development of intelligence in control.

Socialism, Communism, Marxism would seem to be irrelevant to the industrial events of the twentieth century. These doctrines probably express the workers' desire to recapture something of the lost human solidarity. Russian communism, however, although it claims this purpose, seems to be expressive of twentieth-century methods rather than of an ideal of human solidarity. The violent uprooting of peasants and workers to take them to a distant scene, the quick and final determination of disputes, are in part perhaps Slavonic and in part due to the critical nature of the present developmental phase. But the conceptions of work and industrial organization which such methods express are more nearly related to the engineering logic of the twentieth century than to Marx's dictatorship of the proletariat. Indeed, if the predictions of engineers have any value, we are about to enter upon an era in which our material production will be accomplished by machines directed by engineers, and the worker, as we at present conceive him, no longer needed by industry. If this is to be, then history will record not the triumph but the extinction of the proletariat. And communist theories of revolution will be superseded by the profoundest revolution mankind has ever contemplated—the development of a society in which there will be no place for the illiterate or the ignorant.

But these ideas are fantastic. The urgent problem of the present is that our administrative *élite* has become addict of a few specialist studies and has unduly discounted the human and social aspects of industrial organization. The immediate need is to restore effective human collaboration; as a prerequisite of this, extension of the type of research I have reported is the major requirement. An administrator in these days should be qualified as a "listener"; many of our *élite* are so qualified, but are not able to relate the various "echoes" they catch in conversation to anything beyond their own experience. However wise the man, however wide his experience, the limitation to his own experience and his own reflective powers makes him illiterate in comparison with what he might have been with knowledge of the relevant researches. As McDougall has pointed out, the most melancholy fact of our time is that the appropriate inquiries—biological, anthropological—are so little developed that their findings are relatively unavailable for the training of an administrative *élite*. England has for some time required her younger colonial officials to study anthropology—and that is all that can be reported for the world of the twentieth century.

A human problem which is at present even more urgent than that of the general relationship between management and employee is that indicated by former President Hoover in the word "confidence." If confidence can be restored the normal consumption of commodities will be resumed, the price level will rise, the wheels of industry will again begin to turn. But the devices suggested for such restoration are either those which presume an expert knowledge of economics in everyone, or else are of the nature of tricks and shifts which bear a remarkable resemblance to primitive magic. Here again there is a problem in human coöperation which our administrative leaders do not understand. Yet there is evidence available with respect to the locus of the difficulty. When England went off the gold standard in September, 1931, there was much excitement outside England but none in England itself. Confidence was not disturbed, the price level of commodities for the householder remained steady at the time and has been stable since. The cost of living has not changed in England itself—this in the face of considerable variations in the foreign exchange value of the pound. Does anyone believe that an unexpected abandonment of the gold standard in the United States would have so little effect, would cause no visible tremor in the social life of the country? [8] In what respect do the two great nations differ? One cannot answer this except to say that in England to a much larger extent than in the United States the social code is still undamaged. There has been no high mobility of labor, no problem of alien "colonies" and cultures. In spite of a certain *anomie* the social life has not lost its inertia—its capacity to go on—a disadvantage when quick industrial adaptation is required, an advantage in times of social crisis.

Yet the assumption that social codes anywhere, even

[8] This lecture was given in Boston on the evening of March 3rd, 1933.

in England, will continue to operate in their effective non-logical fashion is not justifiable. The world over we are greatly in need of an administrative *élite* who can assess and handle the concrete difficulties of human collaboration. As we lose the non-logic of a social code, we must substitute a logic of understanding. If at all the critical posts in communal activity we had intelligent persons capable of analyzing an individual or group attitude in terms of, first, the degree of logical understanding manifest; second, the non-logic of social codes in action, and, third, the irrational exasperation symptomatic of conflict and baffled effort; if we had an *élite* capable of such analysis, very many of our difficulties would dwindle to vanishing point. Our leaders tend to state these problems in terms of systematic economics, and since the gravamen of the issue is human and social and not primarily economic their statements are not relevant. But no university in civilization offers any present aid to the discovery and training of the new administrator.

In the field of international relations—Sir Arthur Salter's problem—a similar situation exists. In every national group the leaders decry the rising tide of "economic nationalism"—the attempt of every political unit to become economically self-sufficient and independent of the others. Yet the tendency develops unchecked; our leaders, interrupted in speeches deploring the disharmony, are forced to act in a manner that accentuates it. The very descriptions published of the economic consequences of this social malady seem to develop the malady. Here also attention is being given to tariffs, currencies, price level, to anything rather than the discovery of means whereby the human capacity to collaborate may be restored.

The statement of this problem in the international field immediately suggests Geneva and the League of Nations. An ardent supporter of the League, Professor Alfred Zimmern, in a book published in 1928 when League affairs were more promising than now, says: "Has the establishment of a League of Nations ensured the peace of the world? Has it mastered the forces making for disorder? Has it set to work to deal methodically, in the spirit of Science, with the germs of future conflict? Every well-informed observer of international politics must reluctantly answer these questions in the negative." A little later, Zimmern adds: "Every three months some of the leading statesmen of the world assemble at Geneva. What do they do there? Are they free to consider the general interests of mankind? Can they plan to recover control over events? Can they set to work to transform civilization from an appearance to a reality? No doubt, as men of reason and feeling, they would earnestly desire to do so; but, as every one knows, in actual fact they are obliged to spend their efforts upon matters of far lesser significance." [9] Zimmern's reasons for this ineffective outcome of a gallant attempt are odd. He attributes the failure in some rather incomprehensible fashion to Science. He says "the control that Science has so carelessly abandoned has found no one equipped to accept it" (p. 80). And in this connection he speaks of "the abdication of Mind." Elsewhere he claims that Science has given all her attention to the "how" and has forgotten the "why" (p. 76), that science has confused "means" with "ends" (p. 84). What he is probably trying to say is that Geneva would have done better to create and

[9] "Learning and Leadership," Alfred Zimmern, Oxford University Press, p. 81.

foster scientific research—biological and social—than to institute political secretariats. France's reiterated demand for "security," for example, has always been interpreted politically in the environs of Geneva as intended to restrict German activity and growth. No doubt the claim has often had this intent, especially in the years immediately after 1918. But the prime source of the French claim is to be found in the nature of French society. In a recently published book, Mr. E. D. Schoonmaker says: "Somehow in France, to a degree unequalled in any other country, the unity of life has been preserved. And this unity has been achieved with no loss of variety. It is not a unity brought about by conformity, but by a unity of elements held together by the ideal. The colors are there but there is also harmony. . . ." [10] This is a literary expression, but is descriptive of the fact that France, better than any other civilized country, has held her social integrity against the modern drive towards social disorganization. The writer further illustrates this by pointing to the surprising continuity of French foreign policy through extensive changes of political organization during two hundred years. It is this tenacity of social integration which gives the individual Frenchman his feeling of security and solidarity with his group. This tenacity of social integration is the only real source of security, "confidence" and "solidarity" for any people; it is not surprising that the French, uneasy at the signs of social disorganization in the world outside, should preach to others the doctrine of solidarity and its consequent "security." Zimmern probably intends to claim that Geneva has done little or nothing to extend our knowl-

[10] "Our Genial Enemy, France," E. D. Schoonmaker, Ray Long and R. R. Smith.

edge by research into, for example, the sources of national attitude. These sources are rooted in unreason as in reason; both are important to the administrator.

The accomplishment of Geneva must not be belittled. The League has, it is said, provided "a clearing-house of opinion"; it has insisted upon international political discussion. It remains a tragedy that limitation of its appointments to diplomatic and civil service persons has prevented it from doing more. Our administrative *élite*, at Geneva as elsewhere, is the *élite* of yesterday. It faces the problems of the present with the outworn weapons—political and economic theories—of yesterday. The chief difficulty of our time is the breakdown of the social codes that formerly disciplined us to effective working together. For the non-logic of a social code the logic of understanding—biological and social—has not been substituted. The situation is as if Pareto's circulation of the *élite* had been fatally interrupted—the consequence, social disequilibrium. We have too few administrators alert to the fact that it is a human social and not an economic problem which they face. The universities of the world are admirably equipped for the discovery and training of the specialist in science; but they have not begun to think about the discovery and training of the new administrator.

INDEX TO AUTHORS

INDEX TO TOPICS